T0065784

GIVE
US
THIS
DAY

THE LORD'S PRAYER

TOM KINGERY

WESTBOW
PRESS®
A DIVISION OF THOMAS NELSON
& ZONDERVAN

WestBow Press books may be ordered through booksellers or by contacting:

WestBow Press
A Division of Thomas Nelson & Zondervan
1663 Liberty Drive
Bloomington, IN 47403
www.westbowpress.com
844-714-3454

Scripture quotations marked KJV are taken from the Holy Bible, King James Version (Authorized Version). First published in 1611. Quoted from the KJV Classic Reference Bible, Copyright © 1983 by The Zondervan Corporation.

Scriptureare taken from the New Revised Standard Version of the Bible, Copyright © 1989, by the Division of Christian Education of the National Council of the Churches of Christ in the United States of America. Used by permission. All rights reserved.

ISBN: 978-1-6642-9010-5 (sc)
ISBN: 978-1-6642-9011-2 (e)

Library of Congress Control Number: 2023901058

Print information available on the last page.

WestBow Press rev. date: 02/03/2023

PREFACE

Our Father, who art in heaven,
hallowed be thy name;
thy kingdom come;
thy will be done; on earth as it is in heaven.
Give us this day our daily bread.
And forgive us our trespasses,
as we forgive those who trespass against us.
And lead us not into temptation; but deliver us from evil.
For thine is the kingdom and the power and the glory
forever.
Amen.
—Matthew 6:9–13 (KJV, Traditional)

Prayer is the poetry of the soul.

There is no shortage of books about the Lord's Prayer. And being from the Department of Redundancy Department, I will apologize for adding one more. But it seemed relevant to me to let the light of my understanding shine since every offering on this well-known prayer is filtered through the lenses of their authors, and I am one more lens. My focus may be different in some degree than that of others, and what I have to say about prayer in general can, I believe, be useful. It won't hurt anyone to read another studied exposition of The Prayer, and I offer this work as a simple gift from my heart. Please, receive it as you wish. I hope you can feel the power of this prayer as I have. It is an inspiration even as it is sadly taken for granted because it has been memorized and repeated so often that it seems to lose its meaning. Here is what it means to me, and I hope what it can mean for you.

Each chapter of this book will begin with a few paragraphs about what prayer can be, how and why we pray, and what place prayer can have in the life of those who believe. As with any offering from any writer, what you see here is a piece of my heart. And I want to share it.

A Psalm—A Piece of David's Heart

As a deer longs for flowing streams, so my soul longs for you, O God. My soul thirsts for God, for the living God. When shall I come and behold the face of God? My tears have been my food, day and night, while people say to me continually, "Where is your God?" These things I remember, as I pour out my soul: how I went with the throng and led them in procession to the house of God, with glad shouts and songs of thanksgiving, a multitude keeping festival. Why are you cast down, O my soul, and why are you disquieted within me? Hope in God; for I shall again praise him, my help and my God. My soul is cast down within me; therefore, I remember you from the land of Jordan and of Hermon, from Mount Mizar. Deep calls to deep at the thunder of your cataracts; all your waves and your billows have gone over me. By day the Lord commands his steadfast love, and at night his song is with me, a prayer to the God of my life. I say to God, my rock, "Why have you forgotten me? Why must I walk about mournfully because the enemy oppresses me?" As with a deadly wound in my body, my adversaries taunt me, while they say to me continually, "Where is your God?" Why are you cast down, O my soul, and why are you disquieted within me? Hope in God; for I shall again praise him. (Psalm 42:1–11)

INTRODUCTION

The Lord is near to all who call on him,
to all who call on him in truth.
—Psalm 145:18

Prayer in General

Prayer is both an outward act of communication and an inner act of communion. It is an external act of encounter and an inner state of penetration. What prayer becomes is an outward expression of an inward state of being. E. Stanley Jones has said that "prayer is not so much an act as an attitude."

I like to say that prayer is the poetry of the soul.

Prayer, as an attitude, bears a threefold relationship: toward self, with God, and with the world. But more than anything else, prayer is what makes us, as human beings, the image and likeness of God, because when we are praying, we are spiritual beings trying to connect to the Spirit of God. Often prayer includes simply presenting ourselves before the presence of God.

Prayer is used in many ways. Some use prayer like a hand-railing on the stairs—they use it only when they need it, and then, only when it's hard to get up. Some use prayer like a parachute—it's always there, but it's only used if they need it, and even then, only when they're falling. Some use prayer like a night-light—they need it to see how to get through the darkness; but they don't want to really open their eyes completely, otherwise they'd wake up all the way. And some use prayer like a frying pan—they need it only when they're hungry.

Prayer, at its simplest, is talking to God. Some consider prayer to be self-talk, when you want to give yourself a little boost. Some people see talking to themselves as a matter of getting an expert opinion! To pray is like being a cheerleader to some. To others, it's plugging in. And when you go to the lamp, and the light doesn't turn on, you don't claim that there is no electricity, but you realize that either the bulb is burned out or there's something wrong with the lamp.

Sometimes, the moment of prayer doesn't come until we're desperate ... Like the man who called the fire department and said, "Hurry! My house is on fire!"

And the fireman asked, "Where are you?"

"I'm ... in the kitchen talking on the phone!"

"No, no ... How do we get there?"

"Don't you still have those big red trucks?"

There is a fire burning for each of us; we feel the heat, we see the smoke signals, and eventually we'll realize the need to call on God to save us. God doesn't have a big red truck, though.

Give Us This Day

Let's begin a study of Our Lord's Prayer entitled "Give Us This Day." For each chapter, the focus will be on a different portion of the prayer. This is a key prayer for the Christian church. Everywhere we go, in almost every church we enter, the "Our Father" is recited in one form or another. It is a universal Christian prayer.

Prayer has become an important social issue in our day, and in the context of this study, I would also like to briefly share some of my understanding of the meaning of prayer at the beginning of each chapter, as I have already done with this introduction. Prayer is important. It can be very personal, and it can do a great deal for an individual's faith journey, but it is also something that can be done corporately, together. That is why we have political debates concerning audible prayer in school and public places. My opinion concerning this issue will be lifted as my understanding of the act of prayer is shared.

The bottom line is I'm not in favor of it, though it's not wrong. In Psalm 145:18, we are told, "The Lord is near to all who call on him, to all who call on him in truth." In schools, many of the children may rarely call on God in truth. Sorry to say.

There is, however, one prayer that Christ has told us to pray. We call it "Our Lord's Prayer," because Jesus is our Lord. It is also known as the "Our Father." When we look at the whole prayer, found in Matthew chapter 6, we see seven petitions, or requests, or desires. The first three concern God: God's Nature—hallowed be Thy Name; God's kingdom—Thy kingdom come; and God's will—that it will be done. The other four are concerned with *our* needs: our daily bread; our forgiveness, our defense against temptation, and our deliverance. And a doxology has been tacked on to the end, though it is not included in the passage of scripture, unless it is a later edition.

For now, I would like to focus on the heading and the first petition: Our Father, who art in heaven, hallowed be Thy name!

Our Father

What does it mean to call God Father? First, we know God is not a man. Sometimes, the prayer is changed to be inclusive, and it starts out saying, "Our Creator." But when Jesus began by saying "Our Father," we know He is talking to *His* Father. Jesus is The Son of God. He has a very special relationship with God. But *we* are to address God also as *our* Father. *We* are included in this special relationship. If God is *our* Father, *we*, who speak this prayer, are all His children, and everyone else is our brothers and sisters … one family. In having us say "our Father," not only do we claim to belong to God, but to each other!

For those who claim to be unable to call God Father, either because of some degree of feminism, or because the idea of "father" is a harsh term for them because of an ungracious or abusive earthly father, let's just remember that we are thinking in terms of a *divine* father, a heavenly father, a perfect father, so the image we should hold in our hearts when we pray this prayer is not of a glorified earthly idea, but of an earthly term magnified into divine proportions. We are praying to God and relating to Jesus as our *Brother*. And again, consider the notion of how Jesus is claiming we are His family, where God has adopted us. Paul calls this beautiful reality to mind in Romans 8: "All who are led by the Spirit of God are children of God. For you did not receive a spirit of slavery to fall back into fear, but you have received the spirit of adoption. When we cry, 'Abba! Father!' it is that very Spirit bearing witness with our spirit that we are children of God, and if children, then heirs, heirs of God, and joint heirs with Christ" (14–17). Of course, we need to be aware that we are to "call on him in truth" (Psalm 145:18b).

Saying "our" is also significant. It should not be taken too lightly. It is important with respects to who we are when we pray these words together. Think for a moment about who *we* are. Sometimes we might not consider ourselves a part of *us*. Note, however, the word us is repeated throughout the prayer. But I don't think Jesus ever intended for anyone to change the words to "*my* Father," or "give *me* this day *my* daily bread." We are not alone! We are part of an *us*!

Reasons why some people aren't a part of *us* when we pray this prayer can vary. They just might not feel like a part of the family, even though they sincerely want God's kingdom to come, His will to be done, and all the rest for themselves and others. But a lot of independent believers have a dislike for organized religion. The structure of the institutional church bothers them, or, perhaps, they just don't understand the sinfulness of all the other churchgoing believers, not realizing that the church was always intended for the sinful and the lost. That's why we have the season of Lent every year to remind us that we are, in fact, sinful and lost. Any church that claims to have no sinners is so heavenly minded that they are probably no earthly good.

The church is the Body of Christ. There is a unity, yet there is a vast plurality. Despite differences, we can still say, *our*. Think not only of *the* church, or, a church, but just church. To say *Our Father* is to be a part of church as much as it means being a family member. And above all, remember that it is Jesus, the son of God, who says *Our*, with us. He is Our *Brother*! God is *Our Father*!

Who Art in Heaven

Mark Twain told the story of how Miss Watson, the sister of the Widow Douglas, had been reminding Huckleberry Finn to be a good boy so he can go to heaven. Huck says, "She went and told me all about the good place (heaven). She said all a body would have to do there was go around all day long with a harp and sing forever and ever. So I didn't think much of it. But I never said so. I asked her if she reckoned Tom Sawyer would go there, and she said, not by a considerable sight. I was glad about that because I wanted me and him to be together."

Miss Watson makes heaven sound like a place for musicians and singers. But I think she was only appealing to the beauty of its glory.

The Nicene Creed states the belief that Christ ascended to heaven. But which way is divine? Which way is eternity? Which way is the spiritual dimension? It is not necessarily *up*—in the sky—but *beyond*. Eternity is beyond time and space. Heaven is beyond, but not *out there*. It is within, but not just *inside* of us. A lot of people have only a vague understanding of what heaven might be like, and it's easy to be confused. In Luke 17:21, Christ Himself tells us it is in our midst! Heaven is eternal, divine, perfect, glorious. That's where God is, where God comes from.

Hallowed Be Thy Name

Luke 10:17—The Name is used in healing people. The seventy returned and told Jesus that even the demons were subject to them in His Name!

John 12:13—The Name is used in praise. On Palm Sunday, people sang hosannas saying, "Blessed is He who comes in the name of the Lord!"

John 14:13—It is used in prayer. "Whatever you ask in My Name, I will do it."

Matthew 28:19—Even in baptism, we use the Name. Everyone is baptized in the Name of the Father and of the Son and of the Holy Spirit.

This First petition of the Lord's Prayer invokes the hope to keep God's Name holy, sacred, hallowed. We should give it glory, praise. If only this was always on everyone's mind, no other prayers would ever have to be spoken. Note that God's Name is not made holy only when we pray for it to be kept holy. God's Name is already holy. Our purpose, and the reason we pray for it, is to do our part in hallowing God's Name.

The Name of God is YHWH. Throughout the Old Testament scriptures, it is always substituted with LORD or GOD simply because the Name was traditionally too sacred to pronounce, or even write, mostly because it was presumed to be true that to say the *name* was to cause God to become present. And that could be a dangerous thing for some. The Name of God was first learned by Moses: "I Am" (Exodus 3:13–15). The actual translation of the Hebrew word could mean "causes to be," or, "the One who Is." But it is more progressive in tense and could even mean "Being."

This is the Name of God. It is meant to be kept holy. It is not to be used in vain. Swearing that invokes God, or God's Name, is used more in desperation and aggravation, as well as in ignorance, than with the true intent of invoking God's presence. I think if God appeared every time the swearing invocation was used, a lot of people would be very badly burned.

Remember:

> The Lord is near to all who call on him,
> to all who call on him in truth.
> (Psalm 145:18)

You can tell a lot about how someone feels about us the way they use our name. At one time, my friends were able to describe certain unusual moments by saying, "That's a Kingery!" Now, I hear, "Reverend Kingery!" Sometimes, I feel like saying, "Who?" Many of us can remember the recorded dialogue between the voices of a man and a woman who only spoke one another's names. I believe their names were John and Marcia.

Certain names evoke certain feelings: Hitler; Gandhi; Barack; Newt. The name Thomas means twin, literally. Even the name Jesus, or just the word Christ, evokes special feelings, But people show how they feel about God by the way they use God's name. What we need to learn is that when we say the Name, everything that Name might mean and everything that Name reminds us to do and be is included in that simple utterance. That's why we pray to *hallow* God's Name. Even the way God's Name is used and described in the Revelation of John evokes a sense of power: "On His robe and on His thigh, He has a Name inscribed. ... King of kings and Lord of lords!" (Revelation 19:16). The shield and sword of the Christian soldier are the name of Christ. We bear His name, and we need nothing more. That's why we can sing, "Take the Name of Jesus with you." And that also why we must "All hail the power of Jesus's Name!"

Scriptures

To discover more about what the Bible says about prayer and the Name of God, here are some scripture passages that will help to inspire us:

> I tell you, whatever you ask for in prayer, believe that you have received it, and it will be yours. (Mark 11:24)

> Likewise the Spirit helps us in our weakness, for we do not know how to pray as we ought, but that very Spirit intercedes with sighs too deep for words. (Romans 8:26)

> Let your gentleness be known to everyone. The Lord is near. Do not worry about anything, but in everything by prayer and supplication with thanksgiving let your requests be made known to God. And the peace of God, which surpasses all understanding, will guard your hearts and your minds in Christ Jesus. (Philippians 4:5–7)

> Devote yourself to prayer; keeping alert in it with thanksgiving. (Colossians 4:2)

> Humble yourselves before the Lord, and he will exalt you. (James 4:10)

> Are any among you suffering? They should pray. (James 5:13a)

> The prayer of the righteous is powerful and effective. (James 5:16b)

> Pray without ceasing. (1 Thessalonians 5:17)

> Ask, and it shall be given you; search, and you will find; knock, and the door will be opened for you. For everyone who asks receives, and everyone who searches finds, and for everyone who knocks, the door will be opened. (Matthew 7:7–8)

If in my name you ask me for anything, I will do it. (John 14:14)

Let us therefore approach the throne of grace with boldness, so that we may receive mercy and find grace to help in time of need. (Hebrews 4:16)

And this is the boldness we have in him, that if we ask anything according to his will, he hears us. (1 John 5:14)

First of all, then, I urge that supplications, prayers, intercessions, and thanksgivings be made for everyone. (1 Timothy 2:1–2)

What to Do

Pray. Call on God. Call on God "in truth."

If you haven't memorized the Lord's Prayer, do so now.

See yourself as part of the *us* in this prayer, with God as a perfect, divine Father, and Jesus as a perfect, holy Brother.

Think of how you have used prayer.

Think of what it would mean to make God's Name holy—to hallow it.

Think of the various understandings of "heaven." How do you define "heaven"?

Think about what it means to be spiritual.

Think: How can prayer be like "the poetry of the soul"?

Think of how prayer is an encounter.

A Prayer

Almighty God, help me know that You want me to pray. Help me believe you hear me. You know even the thoughts of my heart. And help me to ask always for Your will to be done, Your way to be revealed, and Your truth to be manifested to the whole world. This I ask in Jesus's name. Amen.

A Poem

Inspiration
If I could bottle inspiration
    and let you have a single taste,
and you could swallow it somehow
    and feel the way its presence graced
        your inner being with its power
        and stirred your heart for just one hour,

Then you would know, in part, or whole
what writes the poetry of the soul,

To catch that star with just a thought
    and let its brilliance be a word
would stagger an enlightened mind
    and give a voice to what's unheard
        but calls out somehow from within
        as heaven's harmonies begin,

then other hearts would start to lift
and know that sweet poetic gift,

And if every heart could see this day
The poetry of their souls would play.

Chapter 1

THY KINGDOM COME

God's divine power has given us everything
needed for life and godliness,
through the knowledge of him who called us
by his own glory and goodness.
Thus he has given us, through these things, his
precious and very great promises,
so that through them you may escape from the corruption
that is in the world because of lust,
and become participants of the divine nature.
For this very reason,
you must make every effort to
support your faith with goodness,
and goodness with knowledge,
and knowledge with self-control,
and self-control with endurance,
and endurance with godliness,
and godliness with mutual affection,
and mutual affection with love.
For if these things are yours and are increasing among you,
they keep you from being ineffective and unfruitful
in the knowledge of our Lord Jesus Christ.
For anyone who lacks these things is short-sighted and blind,
and is forgetful of the cleansing of past sins.
Therefore, brothers and sisters,

be all the more eager to confirm your call and election,
for if you do this, you will never stumble.
For in this way, entry into the eternal kingdom
of our Lord and Savior Jesus Christ
will be richly provided for you.
—2 Peter 1:3–11

The Self in Prayer

Prayer must be seen, first, as an attitude toward ourselves. It is an awareness of who we are, why we are, and what we want to be and do. Prayer is an inner act of communion with ourselves and an inner state of penetration into our utmost being. Prayer is looking inward toward the presence of God in our own souls.

God is always present to us, whether we know it or not. Prayer, then, becomes a surrender to God's summons. We present ourselves to God's presence. In doing so, we become alone in the world as did Jesus when He sought solitude to pray. As we look inward toward God within us, we need to examine ourselves and become aware of our attitudes and our truest needs. In a manner of speaking, we must turn and come face-to-face with our very souls. We can ask ourselves what gives our lives meaning and thereby come to our own personal identities. We can cleanse ourselves of our unhealthy attitudes and vain desires by seeing what we really do need and by seeing what life really is to us. This way, we become transfigured to our true selves, and we begin to be the image and likeness of God.

In prayer, we acknowledge the needs of the eternal souls we encounter, and we learn that we ought to live according to *those* needs and not the selfish wants or desires of our own earthly wills. By praying, we discover the right attitude toward life that would become most conducive to fulfilling the needs of our souls. In prayer, we can begin to know ourselves. This is important: How can we begin to know God until we can know ourselves, until we can know the self that wants to know God? And how can we make any requests, any valid requests, of God before we even begin to know God? Well, I guess you can, but it would be like asking for something from a stranger. The actual reason we can ask God to meet our needs before we really know Him is because God is so loving that He will let us ask, because He knows *us*. And sometimes He will even give us blessings before we ask. But knowing who we are, why we are, and what we want to be and do helps us to know when our unhealthy attitudes and vain desires are in the way of the growth of our spiritual lives, the lives of our souls. We are the children of God. We are here to respond to the life around us, support it, and nurture that life toward its fullness to glorify God.

In prayer we are seeking the will to do this. But the will we seek comes from beyond us. And that is why we pray, "Thy will be done."

Give Us This Day

This is the second petition in the Lord's Prayer. In the introduction, we examined the words, "Our Father, who art in heaven, hallowed be Thy Name." A little girl came up to me after worship one Sunday and asked, "Why do we pray for our name to be Harold?" I didn't quite understand what she meant, so I asked her when she had heard us pray for our name to be Harold. She simply said, "Our Father, who's Art in heaven, Harold be my name." Well, I told her that that was part of a prayer that was spoken with words that were sort of old fashioned. And I said that it was like saying, "Our Father, You are in heaven. I want your name to be *holy*." She seemed satisfied until I heard her ask, "What kind of name is 'Holy'?"

We pray these words so often that we need to stop on occasion and think about what they really mean. I have said that prayer becomes a penetration into the self. In prayer, we begin to know who we are. This is a part of prayer, but prayer includes much more. To really present ourselves before God, we must shed ourselves, let go of our pretenses about who we think we are or are trying to be, and come face-to-face with our souls. Therefore prayer needs to include silence sometimes. And that is why prayer is considered an attitude. If the wrong attitude is stirring within, prayer remains ineffective. That is one of the reasons why public prayer in schools seems unnecessary to me. Prayer needs to be taken seriously for it to really be prayer, rather than just a matter of ritual. And when it is not taken seriously, it serves no purposes other than that maybe it sounds good. Prayer should be a real turning. Not only inward but away from self, looking toward God where we find an awareness of His will even beyond our souls.

Thy Kingdom Come

We pray for God's name to be hallowed, for God's kingdom to come, and for God's will to be done on earth. As we pray for God's kingdom to come, God's will *is* being done. And, likewise, as God's will is done, God's kingdom comes. Zacchaeus was looked upon as a sinner in Jericho where he lived. He was too small to see Jesus over the crowds, so he went out of his way and climbed a sycamore tree. Jesus saw the measures the little man had taken and returned equal measure by sharing some time with Zacchaeus at his house. Zacchaeus shared with Jesus his decision to be good. "'Behold, Lord, the half of my goods I give to the poor; and if I have defrauded anyone of anything, I restore it fourfold …' And Jesus said to him, 'Today, salvation has come to this house'" (Luke 19:1–9). The kingdom was coming.

The Will of God

Micah says, "What does the Lord require of you but to do justice and to love kindness, and to walk humbly with your God?" (Micah 6:8). The kingdom comes when we do what is required.

> Is not this the fast that I choose: to loose the bonds of injustice, to undo the thongs of the yoke, to let the oppressed go free, and to break every yoke? Is it not to share your bread with the hungry, and bring the homeless poor into your house; when you see the naked, to cover them, and not to hide yourself from your own kin? Then your light shall spring forth like the dawn, and your healing shall spring up quickly; your vindicator shall go before you, the glory of the Lord shall be your rear guard. Then you shall call, and the Lord will answer; you shall cry for help, and he will say, Here I am. (Isaiah 58:6–9)

The kingdom comes when we set our priorities right.

Jesus also told Zacchaeus that "the Son of Man came to seek and to save the lost" (Luke 19:10). The kingdom comes when the lost are saved!

Second Peter 1:4 says: "He has given us His precious and very great promises, so that through them you may escape the corruption that is in the world because of lust, and may become partakers of the divine nature." The kingdom comes in this way! And we can partake in its blessings! In 2 Peter 1, Peter lists several virtues we should pursue to add to our faith. In 2 Peter 2:5–6, the RSV says "support," the KJV says "add," and the ESV says "supplement." Spiritual growth is relevant. Faith-enriching efforts are never lost. But Peter says, "If these things are yours and are increasing among you, they keep you from being ineffective and unfruitful in the knowledge of our Lord Jesus Christ" (v. 8). My second book explores this passage of scripture, and I express my hope for spiritual growth for all believers. The title of that book is, in fact, *Supplement Your Faith*. I believe it is God's will that we grow in His grace. "He has given us, through these things, his precious and very great promises" (v. 4a). We can become partakers of the divine nature (v. 4b). And we are to pray for God's will to be done on earth!

On Earth as It Is in Heaven

There is an understanding of God's kingdom that it is transcendent. Heaven is often thought of as a completely different dimension, as well as the place where only God reigns. And yet we pray for His kingdom to come on earth. We pray for God's reign to begin now, not later. Often, the way we pray our Lord's Prayer creates a division between the phrases of this petition, as if it is two different things. We pray for God's kingdom to come and God's will to be done, and then, we pray, "On earth as it is in heaven." But we are praying for God's kingdom to come *on earth* and for God's will to be done *on earth* as it is in heaven. There really should be no pause between the words *God's will be done* and *on earth*. It's OK to put a pause between *earth* and *as it is in heaven*, though. I'll say more about this later, when I talk about "Thy will be done." Suffice it to say that God's will is done consistently, obediently, gladly, and joyfully.

But we want God's kingdom to come! What does that really mean? It means we want God's reign to begin while we are alive, while we can experience it, while we are working for it. We don't want it just to be a mystical idea or some vague future hope—although it is in the future for all who believe. We want the experience of the kingdom to be real for us today. We want what is promised in the Revelation of John. We want a new heaven and a new earth. We want the former things to pass away. We want there to be no more pain, no more tears, and no more death (Revelation 21:3–4) *now*. We want and are praying for all of God's promises to be true today. We want God's purposes for His creation to be fulfilled … even now! The second to the last sentence in the Bible is "Amen, Come, Lord Jesus." (Revelation 22:20b) We want Christ to return permanently to reign on earth. But Christ taught His disciples to pray for the kingdom of God to come even before John's vision was given. That kingdom is the primary subject of most of the parables of Jesus. The kingdom of heaven is like wheat that gets gathered in the barn while the weeds are burned. It's like a grain of mustard seed. It's like yeast hidden in a lump of flour. It's like treasure hidden in a field, a merchant in search of fine pearls, a net cast into the sea. It's like lots of things. What is it like for you? These are some of the things we are praying for when we pray for God's kingdom to come. But … God's kingdom's coming is connected, in Christ's prayer, with God's will being done. Next chapter, I'll share more about God's will, and, getting it done!

Scriptures

To discover more about what the Bible says about prayer and the kingdom of God, here are some scripture passages that will help to inspire us:

> Truly I tell you, if two of you agree on earth about anything you ask, it will be done for you by my Father in heaven. For where two or three are gathered in my name, I am there among them. (Matthew 18:19–20)

> Is there anyone among you who, if your child asks for a fish, will give a snake instead of a fish? Or if the child

asks for an egg, will give a scorpion? If you then, who are evil, know how to give good gifts to your children, how much more will your heavenly Father give the Holy Spirit to those who ask him? (Luke 11:11–13)

The Lord will reign for ever and ever. (Exodus 15:18)

Let the heavens be glad, and let the earth rejoice, and let them say among the nations, "The Lord is king!" (1 Chronicles 16:31)

Your throne, O God, endures forever and ever. (Psalm 45:6)

The Lord is king, he is robed in majesty; the Lord is robed, he is girded with strength. He has established the world; it shall never be moved; your throne is established from of old; you are from everlasting. (Psalm 93:1–2)

They shall speak of the glory of your kingdom, and tell of your power, to make known to all people your mighty deeds, and the glorious splendor of your kingdom. Your kingdom is an everlasting kingdom, and your dominion endures throughout all generations. (Psalm 145:11–13)

O Lord of hosts, God of Israel, who are enthroned above the cherubim, you are God, you alone; of all the kingdoms of the earth, you made heaven and earth. (Isaiah 37:16)

Hosanna! Blessed is the one who comes in the name of the Lord—the King of Israel! (John 12:13b)

For a child has been born to us, a son is given to us; authority rests upon his shoulders; and he is named, Wonderful Counselor, Mighty God, Everlasting Father, Prince of Peace. His authority shall grow continually, and there shall be endless peace for the throne of David and his kingdom. He will establish it with justice and with righteousness from this time onward and forevermore. (Isaiah 9:6–7)

To him was given dominion and glory and kingship, that all peoples, nations, and languages should serve him. His dominion is an everlasting dominion that shall not pass away, and his kingship is one that shall never be destroyed. (Daniel 7:14)

As you go, proclaim the good news, "The kingdom of heaven has come near." (Matthew 10:7)

The kingdom of heaven is like a mustard seed that someone sowed in his field; it is the smallest of all the seeds, but when it has grown it is the greatest of shrubs and becomes a tree, so that the birds of the air come and make their nests in its branches. (Matthew 13:31–32)

What to Do

Examine yourself. Part of prayer is encountering the soul within you. What do you find?

Examine your priorities in the light of Isaiah 58:6–9 and Micah 6:8.

Examine your thoughts about God's kingdom.

Think: What will God's kingdom look like when it comes?

Ask yourself: How can I know the will of God?

Think: How do you escape the corruption that is in the world?

Support your faith with goodness, knowledge, self-control, endurance, godliness, mutual affection, and love. (2 Peter 1:5–7)

A Prayer

Almighty God, I trust the vision of Your kingdom. My heart thrills at the beauty of its glory. My soul feeds on the eternal quality of your dominion and your reign. I long to be with You there. It will be a privilege to enter it and an honor to be with You. It gives me joy just to think of such a possibility. Help me live for it now and walk in the spirit of Your love. This I ask in Jesus's name. Amen.

A Poem

Make Clear a Vision
Make clear a vision of Your kingdom, my Lord,
Where You're perfectly present, and loved, and adored.
Help it to raise in my heart a great hope
that comforts me now as I reach, and I grope
for a sliver of blessing, a morsel of grace
as I battle the troublesome demons I face.

By all You have given and all I have learned
and all it ignites in me—sparks have returned
as I call to remembrance Your most perfect fire
illuminating scenes of my greatest desire
I see heaven revealed in my heart and all 'round,
and I can't help but proclaim the vision I've found.

The vision is like a beginning for me.
It opens a pathway for all I will see.

Chapter 2

THY WILL BE DONE

With what shall I come before the Lord, and
bow myself before God on high?
Shall I come before him with burnt offerings, with calves a year old?
Will the Lord be pleased with thousands of rams,
with ten thousands of rivers of oil?
Shall I give my firstborn for my transgressions,
the fruit of my body for the sin of my soul?"
He has shown you, O mortal, what is good;
and what does the Lord require of you but to do justice,
and to love kindness, and to walk humbly with your God?
—Micah 6:6–8

God in Prayer—I have said that prayer is not so much an act as an attitude. And I have said that it is in one sense an attitude toward self, an awareness of who we are, why we are, and what we want to be and do. Knowing ourselves is important, for how can we begin to know God until we can begin to know ourselves? Once, however, we have penetrated within and come face-to-face with our very own soul, we can then begin to look toward God. Prayer, as an attitude, then, becomes concerned with our relationship with God. Prayer, therefore, becomes an external act of encounter and a purposeful expression of dependence. Prayer becomes a response of commitment and a reaching in hope. It is a glance beyond ourselves toward the universal presence of the Being of God.

Not only from an inward glance do we find the presence of the being of God but also, and perhaps even more so, in an outward glance upon God's great creation. Reflecting on the wonders of life in the world we see, we cannot help but become aware of the presence of God. It is not only in the life cycle of nature but in the life-filled cities and towns, which have been called centers of life. Seeing life in the world, we turn to God with the belief that without Him, without His will, there would be nothing. We become able to acknowledge God in, or through, everything we see. Every encounter with life becomes a communion. Every sight reveals God's presence, God's touch.

The relationship with God through prayer becomes a response to life, and to life's very basic needs. Prayer is a dedication to the life not just within our own souls but in all creation. Even in the distortion of violence and the throes of death, our commitment becomes a hope. Prayer is the attitude of dedication and commitment, without which the act of prayer is left empty. Some advocate public prayer in schools and elsewhere because that would be the only instance for many to know or experience God to some degree. But for those who are not taught faith outside of school, prayer would remain as only words without meaning. Prayer needs dedication and commitment, sincerity, for the words and hopes spoken to be true prayer.

Prayer is being attentive to the will of God and intentional in our response. Prayer is an anticipation for life to be shared in a more communal way. Prayer becomes an outward meeting of God in all life. It becomes an attitude that everything we do can be a form of communion. Prayer is a seeking and a reaching for God, not just inwardly but outwardly as well. As God is universally present, we can constantly present ourselves to His Presence. But even more so, prayer creates an awareness of our communal needs and an effort to see them met.

Give Us This Day—A man once told me that he didn't need to pray because he never did anything wrong. When I asked him if he had ever prayed just to thank God for His good guidance, he said no, I knew he didn't really know much about prayer, and I shared with him a little bit of what I understood, because I believe prayer is more than something we do just for ourselves. We can pray for the needs of others, which means not only that we have certain hopes for them but that we want guidance as to how to fulfill those needs.

Thy Kingdom Come—It comes when basic needs can be fulfilled. Thy will be done. The kingdom comes in the act, the doing, the fulfilling of those needs. Prayer is not just a matter of hoping for those needs to be fulfilled; being a part of the kingdom includes being a part of fulfilling needs. Prayer gets us in touch with those needs and with the will to supply them, to meet those needs. Those needs are not just supplied passively the way our nose supplies air for our lungs, but actively, the way a window or a vent needs to be opened for air to pass through. And speaking of needs and noses, the reason elephants need such a large trunk is because they have no glove compartments! Needs. Our first need, and perhaps most relevant of all, is to discover God's will … and do it!

Thy Will Be Done—Knowing God's will, then, we need to begin to see that it must be done on earth. Not done just in bits and pieces, but as it is in heaven, where the will of God is done constantly, consistently, completely, and gladly. But how do we build that bridge between knowing and doing the will of God?

Part of the answer comes in lifting just two simple words from this part of the Lord's Prayer: *be done*! Too often, the emphasis is on *will* and *knowing* the will. But God's kingdom doesn't come, and God's name is never hallowed just because people know His will. His will must be *done* (Matthew 7:21, 24). Doing it gives us the building blocks for that bridge. Jesus tells His disciples that "whoever would be great among you must be your servant, and whoever would be first among you must be slave of all. For the Son of Man also came not to be served but to serve, and to give His Life as a ransom for many" (Mark 10:44–45).

The Will of God—What does God want? What are God's desires for His creation? Faith, following Jesus, being a disciple, is a process of learning the will of God. In Genesis, God's will for Adam and Eve was to take care of the garden, to till it and keep it (Genesis 2:15). But God also willed that they stay away from the fruit of the Tree of Knowledge of

Good and Evil. (2:17) After they didn't, though, and sinfulness found its way into the human heart, God's will was to cleanse the earth. "The Lord saw that the wickedness of humankind was great in the earth, and that every inclination of the thoughts of their hearts was only evil continually. And the Lord was sorry that He had made humankind on the earth, and it grieved Him to His heart" (Genesis 6:5–6). So God sent the Flood. Eventually, God called Abraham. "I will make of you a great nation, and I will bless you, and make your name great, so that you will be a blessing." God's will was that Abraham would be blessed and would be a blessing. And I believe *that* is God's will for all humankind—to be blessed and to be a blessing. In Exodus, God gave the Ten Commandments. God's will for us includes His Law, which includes practicing certain behaviors and avoiding others. If you want to know God's will for creation, learn what God has done and continues to do. Micah revealed an understanding of God's will that was explained in a nutshell: to do justice, to love kindness, and to walk humbly with your God (Micah 6:8). God wanted deliverance for the Hebrews in Egypt, and God's will is salvation. So God sent His Son. God became incarnate in Jesus … God came to us, in the past and in the present. "Indeed, God did not send the Son into the world to condemn the world, but in order that the world might be saved through Him!" (John 3:17).

And Jesus came not to be served but to serve. Servanthood is part of the bridge between knowing God's will and doing God's will. What builds that bridge is the act of doing of God's will. Then, we will learn the forgiveness that has come by Christ. Included in 2 Peter 1:3-4, with "the precious and very great promises," is a promise of forgiveness. And we should not want to escape from the corruption that is in the world by escaping from service! To make the escape, we must become prisoners for Christ, bound to His will, serving what is good. Prayer inspires us to connect, to be bound to Christ as Paul was. He felt proud to be a prisoner for Christ (Ephesians 3:1; 4:1). In heaven, God's will is done consistently, obediently, gladly, and joyfully. May God's will be done this way on earth.

"If you do this, you will never fall" (2 Peter 1:5–11). Serving God's will is following the Way, it is following the Truth, it is following Life itself as known in Jesus Christ. It is to "support your faith … with goodness, knowledge, self-control, godliness, endurance, mutual affection, and love" (2 Peter 1:5–7). To do so is to build the bridge that leads to the home where the Father has prepared a place for us. 'If you do this, you will never stumble. For in this way, entry into the eternal kingdom of our Lord and Savior Jesus Christ will be richly provided for you" (2 Peter 1:10). Thy kingdom come!

If you do this! The will of God must become the will of the faithful! Our biggest challenge is that we have our own wills, and we do not automatically know or do God's will. So we need to be transformed so that we can conform our wills to the will of God. More about that later.

Scriptures

To discover more about what the Bible says about prayer and the will of God, here are some scripture passages that will help to inspire us:

> For surely I know the plans I have for you, says the Lord, plans for welfare and not for harm, to give you a future with hope. Then when you will call upon me and come and pray to me, I will hear you. When you search for me, you will find me; if you seek me with all your heart, I will let you find me, says the Lord. (Jeremiah 29:11–14)

> Make me to know your ways, O Lord; teach me your paths. Lead me in your truth, and teach me, for you are the God of my salvation; for you I wait all day long. (Psalm 25:4–5)

> Trust in the Lord with all your heart, and do not rely on your own insight. In all your ways acknowledge him, and he will make straight your paths. (Proverbs 3:5–6)

> Do not be conformed to this world, but be transformed by the renewing of your minds, so that you may discern what is the will of God—what is good and acceptable and perfect. (Romans 12:2)

Do not be foolish, but understand what the will of the Lord is. Do not get drunk with wine, for that is debauchery; but be filled with the Spirit, as you sing psalms and hymns and spiritual songs among yourselves, singing and making melody to the Lord in your hearts, giving thanks to God the Father at all times, and for everything in the name of our Lord Jesus Christ. (Ephesians 5:17–20)

For this is the will of God, your sanctification: that you abstain from fornication. (1 Thessalonians 4:3)

Give thanks in all circumstances; for this is the will of God in Christ Jesus for you. (1 Thessalonians 5:18)

For you need endurance, so that when you have done the will of God, you may receive what was promised. (Hebrews 10:36)

Now may the God of peace who brought back from the dead our Lord Jesus, the great shepherd of the sheep, by the blood of the eternal covenant, make you complete in everything good so that you may do his will, working among us that which is pleasing in his sight, through Jesus Christ, to whom be the glory forever and ever. Amen. (Hebrews 13:20–21)

For it is God's will that by doing right you should silence the ignorance of the foolish. (1 Peter 2:15)

The Lord is not slow about his promise, as some think of slowness, but is patient with you, not wanting any to perish, but all to come to repentance. (2 Peter 3:9)

Strive first for the kingdom of God and his righteousness, and all these things will be given to you as well. (Matthew 6:33)

Whoever does the will of God is my brother and sister and mother. (Mark 3:35)

If any want to become my followers, let them deny themselves and take up their cross daily and follow me. (Luke 9:23)

For I have come down from heaven, not to do my own will, but the will of him who sent me. And this is the will of him who sent me, that I should lose nothing of all that he has given me, but raise it up on the last day. This is indeed the will of my Father, that all who see the Son and believe in him may have eternal life, and I will raise them up on the last day. (John 6:38–40)

What to Do

Feel the need to pray … even if it is just to say, "Thanks!"

Act on your faith. Faith is not just a matter of knowing something. It includes doing something.

Ask yourself, "What does God want?" Make a list.

Consider the ways your will can get in the way of God's will.

Consider some of the ways you have been blessed. How can you be a blessing?

Think: How can you support your faith with the virtues listed in 2 Peter 1:5–7?

Consider what you might pray for on behalf of others.

A Prayer

Almighty God, Your way, Your Truth, Your life are forever before me. Help me to see and know and follow as I strive to do Your holy will. Help me to be as compassionate and merciful, loving and just, forgiving and kind as my Savior. May His glory be revealed in the ways I live my life, in the words I speak, and in the work I do. This I ask in Jesus's Name. Amen.

A Poem

Every Encounter

Every encounter is a communion with chance—
A witness to a glorious but random expanse
That eternity offers and divinity planned
And put in our pathway at heaven's command.
And every experience, every event,
Sees providence acting in how it was sent.

Every inward glance we take
Reveals a truth we cannot break.
We can't deny it; we must accept
All that confronts us as it is kept.

And when we understand our soul—
    That inner depth that in us lives—
We'll gain a vision of our goal
    And all the prayers and dreams God gives.

Chapter 3

OUR DAILY BREAD

When they found him on the other side of the sea, they said to him,
"Rabbi, when did you come here?"
Jesus answered them, "Very truly, I tell you,
you are looking for me, not because you saw signs,
but because you ate your fill of the loaves.
Do not work for the food that perishes,
but for the food that endures for eternal life,
which the Son of Man will give you.
For it is on him that God the Father has set his seal."
Then they said to him, "What must we do
to perform the works of God?"
Jesus answered them, "This is the work of God,
that you believe in him whom he has sent."
So they said to him, "What sign are you going to give us then,
so that we may see it and believe you?
What work are you performing?
Our ancestors ate the manna in the wilderness; as it is written,
'He gave them bread from heaven to eat.'"
Then Jesus said to them, "Very truly, I tell you,
it was not Moses who gave you the bread from heaven,
but it is my Father who gives you the true bread from heaven.
For the bread of God is that which comes down from heaven
and gives life to the world."
They said to him, "Sir, give us this bread always."
—John 6:26–35

The World in Prayer

I have defined prayer as an attitude dealing particularly in relationship with ourselves and with God — both inwardly and outwardly, There is some overlap in the discussions, and it will also be obvious that there is an overlap from the discussion of our outward relationship with God through prayer and our relationship with the world through prayer. This gives evidence to the suggestion that prayer is a process. It is an ongoing dialogue. It is an ever-profounder experience of the divine presence.

Often, however, the effort to pray is not easy. We may not always want to pray, and, even if we did, our praying might, at times, seem empty. There may be little or no sense of the Presence of God for the individual at prayer. We may not find the sense of self-affirmation we hope for, so, at this point, we need to know that we can endure. We are not alone. This is where the fellowship we share in the world can help us. We are not alone in God's heavenly courtroom where we are making requests of the King.

For this very reason—fellowship, public fellowship—is important. Public prayer in school may seem like a good idea to many people. But the fellowship at school is not primarily a spiritual fellowship. Prayer can only attempt to make it so, but public schools are not spiritual institutions; they are secular. They are a place of learning, and much of what is learned is far from subjects in the category of spiritual. Though some might try to claim that everything we learn, all that can be enlightening for the mind, is spiritual. It depends on how you define *spiritual*. I am concerned, here, with the way we relate to God and the Divine. And I believe that prayer obviously includes relating to God. Schools do not automatically create a relationship with God. Either way, I'm not in favor of public prayer in school mainly for the simple reason that most public educators are not really trained in the leading of prayer. And you can't simply use a book, although a book of prayers *can* be very helpful. Schools don't directly teach moral behavior either, for the similar reason that morality is an individual choice. Rules and laws can be taught, but morals are often independent and transcendent of facts and figures. The facts and figures may guide our morals, but they do not create morality. Morality, like prayer, depends more on personal attitudes.

But the fellowships we pursue that are spiritual can help us when it comes to prayer. Like all experiences, the encounter of prayer should be expressed to be understood. And, like any expression of a personal experience, the way we pray is never fully adequate or complete. Thanks to the grace of God, though, our way of praying can change as our experience of a relationship with the Divine, and of the Presence of God deepens. Although prayer may often seem to be a very individual and personal experience, we are not alone. God is with us, and the world is with us, and prayer can become an outward act of communication!

Give Us This Day

One time, a pastor of a church who rarely wore a robe was getting one ready for worship. Asked by one member why, he said he thought the laypeople needed to see what a real minister looked like. And his parishioner said, "Oh, are we going to have a guest preacher?"

Needs. We pray for needs. And one of our daily needs is for bread, food, nourishment, something to sustain us. One of the harsher realities that is part of the attitude of prayer is known in how, as we begin to see ourselves among others who are also in relation to God, and, in seeking the will of God, we might begin to see a lot of the shortcomings of others and of ourselves. Too often, we heap more shortcomings upon others than we admit for ourselves, not quite realizing that we are one of *them* too. We realize that not only do we have needs, but others have needs as well. Daily needs. Likewise, when we are aware that there are others with us, we can realize their blessings, and their hopes for us, for all of *us*.

Daily Bread—Moses and the children of Israel were sustained in the wilderness by the miraculous daily appearance of manna, or bread (Exodus 16:13–15). Isaiah claims that true religion, true worship, includes sharing bread (Isaiah 58:6–7). Bread. In the parable of the Great Judgment in Matthew 25, those who are able to inherit the kingdom of God served Christ by "doing unto the least of these ..." (v. 40) and by responding to a real need: "I was hungry, and you gave me food" (v. 35). Bread. Making bread includes dough, making dough. There's a recipe for Playdough that uses some of the same ingredients that are used for bread. Playdough, clay.

"We are the clay, and Thou (God) art the potter; we are the work of Thy hands" (Isaiah 64:8). God creates us, molds us from the clay that comes from the elements of creation. Bread, our most vital need, is supplied from the same source as the creation of our flesh. Without bread, without food, there would be no flesh. Give us this day *our daily bread*!

Think about all that simple request includes. We are not so fortunate as to have bread miraculously appear as did the Hebrews of the Exodus. It takes many miracles for us to have bread: good soil, seeds, rain, good weather, farmers, mills, flour, other ingredients, ovens, bakers …

Asking God to continually supply the daily need of just bread includes the hope for every part of this miraculous chain of events to be active. Without that chain, without every link in that chain, there would be no food. Give us this day our daily bread!

Bread—in Christ's day, and in Christ's part of the world—could not keep for long. They had no refrigerators or freezers where today we can store supplies for months. Bread became stale in the dryness of the climate, and often in only one day. And certainly, many ailments were very likely to have been caused by eating moldy bread. Remember, too, that the bread of those days was not like our thick, fluffy loaves. It was a bit more flakey, more like crackers or pita bread. But it was food. And it was common. But for many, it was not always common enough. *Give us this day our daily bread.*

This Day—The Lord's Prayer is petitioning, not for an abundance of supplies, but only enough for *this day*. We can only live one day at a time. That's a fact. There is no way for us to fulfill tomorrow's needs today. We can be prepared, but we cannot fulfill the need. This portion of the prayer is a confession of real needs. No one can say they have no needs, and no one can say that tomorrow is really taken care of. That's just a confident feeling because we really don't know what tomorrow will bring. Today … we have *these* needs. Tomorrow's may be different. But the interesting thing about this prayer is that behind the idea of daily bread is the true *Bread of Life*. We need more than food to really live. Warmth and protection against the elements are needed too. And we also have spiritual and emotional needs. These are real needs too. We are sustained by more than food. Give us this day … "Do not be anxious about tomorrow; tomorrow will be anxious for itself" (Matthew 6:25–34). We get so caught up in tomorrow's needs that we lose sight of God's kingdom … today. "Do not be worried (or anxious), saying, 'What shall we eat?' or 'What shall we drink?' or 'What shall we wear?' For the Gentiles seek those things, and your heavenly Father knows you need them all. But seek first His Kingdom and His righteousness, and all these things shall be yours as well" (31–33). Thy kingdom come! The presence of the kingdom includes the provision of these very basic everyday needs. But the kingdom does not come until we seek His righteousness—Thy will be done—and do those things that can fulfill those needs, at least for this day!

Give Us Bread—*Us*—*Our*. It does not say *my* daily bread, and us doesn't mean *my* country or *my* class or *my* race. It includes whoever can call God Father. And to me, that means every human being. We are all God's children, even though some may have run away from home and gotten lost. There's a story about a woman on Thanksgiving Day who had prepared, as do many of us in the United States of America, enough food for an army—or, at least, a great deal more than everyone could eat. And then, aware that most of the people of the world do not even get enough, she prayed, "Forgive us this day our daily bread." Forgive us. Our daily bread is so abundant, while others only survive. That says something about *us*!

"Give us …" It's asking God to provide, and to share. We ask God to share, and then we do not! But one of the greatest examples of sharing comes from the story in scripture where Jesus fed five thousand people. Each one received food somehow. It was a miracle. But then Christ had his disciples gather the leftovers, and twelve baskets, one for each disciple, were filled! Wow! Jesus had given them more than enough. But then He left the people, and they came after Him. Jesus was the great giver of bread!

But He reprimanded these followers: "Truly, truly, I say to you, you seek me not because you saw signs but because you ate your fill of the loaves" (John 6:26). They got the food, but they missed the miracle, the power of God in Jesus—the life-giving power in the One who gives eternal life. Their interest in Christ was concerned more with what He could do for them materially. Christ saw their enthusiasm, but He knew there was a difference between an admirer and a real disciple. He reprimands them because they only wanted a quick fix to satisfy a returning hunger. They didn't want any spiritual nourishment. They didn't really care that Christ could give them eternal nourishment, soul food, feeding their inner needs, their inner hunger.

Christ tells them: "Do not labor for the food which perishes, but for the food which endures to eternal life" (v. 27). And those who followed Him asked, "What must we do?" (v. 28). His response is that finding this special bread comes in belief; Christ is telling us that we need faith as much, if not more, than we need food. He suggests that we must have an appetite for spiritual things. "Labor for the food which endures" (c. 27b). "Seek God's Kingdom and His righteousness, and all these things shall be yours as well" (Matthew 6:33).

These admirers, who had just seen a miracle that fed five thousand people, asked for another sign. It's as if Moses, who did the same sort of thing, was enough for them. They thought Jesus was no different. But He was: "Your ancestors ate manna in the wilderness and they died. This is the Bread which comes down from Heaven, that a man may eat of it and not die!" (John 6:49–50). In John 6:33 we are told, "The Bread of God is that which comes down from Heaven and gives life to the world!"

And they said to Him: "Lord, give us this bread always" (John 6:34). And we pray, "Father ... give us this day our daily bread." Jesus said: "I am the Bread of Life; they who come to Me shall not hunger, and they who believe in Me shall never thirst!" (John 6:35).

Not Bread Alone—Today, there are still people starving. Not only because they don't have food. There are even physically healthy people who are starving spiritually because they just are not aware of their spiritual appetites and needs. They have no emotional hunger because they have no compassion. They have no inner thirst because they are empty. Who are they? Do you know any of them? You do. You should. You can. You are. But remember, the temptations today are much more abundant than the offerings of bread. Bread. Jesus was tempted to turn stones into bread right when He was physically starved. And what did He say? "You shall not live by bread alone, but by every word that proceeds from the mouth of God!" (Matthew 4:4). On what do you live? Are you feeding on the Word of God? Are you nurturing the seeds of faith planted in the soil of your life? Come to Christ, and you will not hunger! Believe in Him, and you will not thirst!

Scriptures

To discover more about what the Bible says about prayer and bread, here are some scripture passages that will help to inspire us:

> By the sweat of your face you shall eat bread until you return to the ground, for out of it you were taken; you are dust, and to dust you shall return. (Genesis 3:19)

> He humbled you by letting you hunger, then by feeding you with manna, which neither you nor your ancestors were acquainted, to make you understand that one does not live by bread alone, but by every word that comes from the mouth of the Lord. (Deuteronomy 8:3)

> You cause the grass to grow for the cattle, and plants for people to use; to bring forth food from the earth, and wine to gladden the human heart, oil to make the face shine, and bread to strengthen the human heart. (Psalm 104:14–15)

> I will satisfy the poor with bread. (Psalm 132:15b)

> Why do you spend your money for that which is not bread, and your labor for that which does not satisfy? (Isaiah 55:2)

> The time is surely coming, says the Lord God, when I will send a famine on the land; not a famine of bread, or a thirst for water, but of hearing the words of the Lord. (Amos 8:11)

While they were eating, Jesus took a loaf of bread, and after blessing it he broke it, gave it to his disciples, and said, "Take, eat, this is my body." (Matthew 26:26)

Is there anyone among you who, if your child asks for bread, will give a stone? (Matthew 7:9)

The kingdom of heaven is like yeast that a woman took and mixed it with three measures of flour until all of it was leavened. (Matthew 13:33)

When the disciples reached the other side, they had forgotten to bring bread. Jesus said to them, "Watch out, and beware of the yeast of the Pharisees and Sadducees." They said to one another, "It is because we have brought no bread." And becoming aware of it, Jesus said, "You of little faith, why are you talking about having no bread? Do you still not perceive? Do you not remember the five loaves for the five thousand, and how many baskets you gathered? Or the seven loaves for the four thousand, and how many baskets you gathered? How could you fail to perceive that I was not speaking about bread? Beware of the yeast of the Pharisees and Sadducees!" Then they understood that he had not told them to beware of the yeast of bread, but of the teaching of the Pharisees and Sadducees. (Matthew 16:5–12)

As it is written, "He scatters abroad, he gives to the poor; his righteousness endures forever." He who supplies seed to the sower and bread for food will supply and multiply your seed for sowing and increase the harvest of your righteousness. (2 Corinthians 9:9–10)

The bread that we break is it not a sharing in the body of Christ? Because there is one bread, we who are many are one body, for we all partake of the one bread. (1 Corinthians 10:16b-17)

As often as you eat this bread and drink this cup, you proclaim the Lord's death until he comes. (1 Corinthians 11:26)

I am the bread of life. (John 6:48)

What to Do

Think about how you relate to others—your *us*.

Consider your needs, and the needs of those you know. You have something to pray for. How do you communicate your needs?

Consider your abundance. How full is your pantry, your cupboard, your refrigerator? Do you have more than your daily needs?

Consider your priorities. What do you "seek first"?

Consider why some people might be "anxious" about their life-sustaining resources. What should we, who have more than enough, be doing for those who don't have enough?

Ask yourself, "How am I spiritually hungry?" "How am I spiritually thirsty?"

Consider: "How am I nurturing the spiritual seeds?"

Consider what it might mean when, in Communion, Jesus called the bread His Body (Matthew 26:26). What does it mean when the church is called the Body of Christ? (1 Corinthians 12:27; Romans 12:5).

A Prayer

Almighty God, You would feed me till I want no more. So make me hungry for Your Word, thirsty for Your truth, eager for Your grace. Make me to know this purpose as my priority. And help me to know that there are many others who also seek Your spiritual blessings. When I pray, help me to do more than intercede for myself, but let me raise up petitions for all my brothers and sisters throughout the world. This I ask in Jesus's Name. Amen.

A Poem

Together
I am not alone. I know you're there.
I've felt your presence. I've heard your prayer.
You made requests for me to heal,
that I might rise from this ordeal
and find new strength and then endure.
It gave me hope when I was unsure.
And I will also pray for you.
There's so much more that we can do
when our hopes can be combined,
and we both think with a single mind.
And there are others who can pray
on our behalf for a better day.
Let's dream together. Let's start a fire,
And ask for things we all desire.

Chapter 4

FORGIVE US OUR TRESPASSES

For if you forgive others their trespasses,
your heavenly Father will also forgive you.
—Matthew 6:14

The World in Prayer—A Fellowship of Faith

As with our moments of self-examination we can become more aware of
who we are, so too, can we gain an awareness through our relation to others.
Sometimes we can see ourselves by seeing how others see us. We do not have
an individual monopoly on life. Life is experienced by all around us. Without
others, we might never know this. We need to accept the fact that the will
of God in our spirits is not unique to us. We need to accept others. We need
to be aware of others. We can experience other encounters that can be just
as inspiring as our individual encounter with God. We can experience the
Presence of God working within our fellow human beings as well as in God's
created universe. In other words, others can inspire us! And we need them.

As we learn to accept the inspiration of God in and through the lives
of others, we can gain fellowship and support. As a part of a community,
we can share ... our prayers, our needs, our hopes, our dreams. And in that
community, we can find unity. There is a power in the harmony that we
can find in fellowship that is often much more tangible than our harmony
with the more one-on-one abstract power of God and God's divine will.

There can come a re-centering of our lives, not in ourselves, but in the universal Presence of God throughout creation, and, especially, within all those who seek to come into God's Presence and say, together, *Our Father.* How wonderful it is to hear a beautiful voice singing words of praise, glorifying God! How incredibly awesome it can be to hear a whole choir! When we come together with others, the praise is magnified, the glory is multiplied, and the purpose of our corporate unity is complemented!

As an attitude in relation to the world, prayer becomes a caring for life, supporting, nurturing, and sharing life in all we do, in all existence, in every moment of being in relation with whatever is not just us, the self. Praying is a way of acknowledging God's presence in others and in every aspect of God's great creation!

So, prayer can become a process of sharing needs and enhancing our personal praise. It can become a process of mutual concentration on the will of God in the world. Prayer becomes the surfacing of problems, either individual or communal, and it is a response—not only in communal thanksgiving but in a hope that problems may be resolved or that goals/ visions may be met. In such a communal system of support, endurance is not just an individual burden. Prayer becomes an opening up of life to the alignment of our will to the will of God, to the inspiration of God within ourselves and in others. And prayer becomes a process of seeking the fulfilling of the needs and expressing the joys we meet in community and of living abundantly.

If one person prayed in worship, or even if there is a community that prays together responsively, there is an alignment of wills to the will of God. When there is a concentration on life, life can become an amazing inspiration, a source of strength. Healing can occur, needs can be fulfilled, and prayers can be answered. We become able to experience the presence of God in eternity beyond us, yet it seems to draw us toward the kingdom around us. It may seem to be only a feeling deep inside, and yet it can be a reality that surrounds us. Either way, prayer becomes an attitude by which we, all of us, live...together.

Give Us This Day

In the fellowship of those who have gathered to pray, as I said previously, we can meet people who have shortcomings. They have needs; they need daily sustenance. But because some shortcomings may go beyond the need for daily bread, we experience moral shortcomings. We don't want to take credit for any shortcomings, but we are not above or better than others. That should become clear to us as we relate more deeply to God. Praying, we also begin to discover how impoverished, how bankrupt, we really are. Some have thought that prayer never brought them any self-improvement. It doesn't. It brings an awareness of the need to improve. Self-inventory gives us a chance to take stock in ourselves, or for filling those empty spaces we might find. Some have believed that to pray was to do nothing. The problem, though, with doing nothing is that you never know when you're finished! What prayer does is help us decide what to do. It doesn't do it for us. Sometimes, prayer simply helps us decide to be patient when nothing can be done. Patience is an important part of prayer. And we must learn to be patient with ourselves as much as we must be patient with others.

Sometimes a way of being patient comes in giving second chances. And to give a second chance, we must be forgiving, merciful.

Forgive Us—This petition of The Lord's Prayer reminds us that we are guilty! When we pray for God to forgive us our trespasses, we are admitting our guilt. We are admitting that we have trespassed; that we are indebted to God. We stand under the conviction that we have failed to hallow God's Name. Not only have we so failed by the sins we commit but by the good we have omitted. The will of God to which we have aligned our wills is left undone! And there is so much to do before the kingdom may come. To be forgiven, we need to repent.

We stand under the conviction of sin. Our relationship with our Father has been torn asunder, and our relationships with our brothers and sisters in God's family are also full of gaping wounds. But forgiveness can provide the sutures to bind those wounds. The Holy Spirit is the surgeon who comes, sometimes, even to cauterize those wounds with fire before we lose too much of our life's blood. And the last thing we should do is pour salt into another's wounds.

Remember that in this prayer, the third person plural is being used: Our, Us, We. Forgive *us* our trespasses! As individuals, we need forgiveness. But we are not alone. Each one of us needs forgiveness. And each one of us, by praying this prayer, is praying for the forgiveness of all. There may be times when we can, in fact, experience corporate guilt, as in classism or racism. A whole group may express prejudice or superiority. This is a sin, and it needs to be overcome. We need to repent, and we need forgiveness. We do not just seek forgiveness for the sake of forgiveness but for the sake of receiving a second chance. But, still, we need to change, or that second chance will result in the same consequences of our evil ways. Forgive us. We all need to change!

In Christ's conclusion, after He has taught His disciples how to pray, He says: "For if you forgive others their trespasses, your heavenly Father also will forgive you; but if you do not forgive others their trespasses, neither will your Father forgive your trespasses" (Matthew 6:14–15). "With the judgment you pronounce you will be judged; and the measure you give will be the measure you get!" (Matthew 7:2). Tune in for more, in the next chapter, when I talk about "*as we forgive …*"

Trespasses/Debts. Forgive us our trespasses. When we trespass, we are not just crossing over the boundaries of someone else's space; we're also reaching beyond our own limitations in a way that leaves us off-balance or that leaves our vision blurred, unable to see the will of God clearly.

Trespasses. Some say debts. Luke's version of the Lord's Prayer says, "Forgive us our sins …" (Luke 11:4). When we regard our sins as debts, sometimes, we can begin to see how bankrupt we've become. Not just me; it says, Forgive *us*! There are both personal sins, such as greed, deceit, lust, dishonesty, and selfishness; and, social sins, such as class pride, racial prejudice, national supremacy, or objectivism. And as we sin, we come under a special spiritual obligation to make amends and are not free until we have fulfilled that obligation, paid that debt. But the interest rates are high. The longer we continue to sin, the deeper that debt may seem. The longer we continue to take that small amount of poison, the more it builds up in our systems, and it will eventually kill us. "Sin, when it is finished, brings forth death!" (James 1:15). And we can't return to our past and make up for our debts because we have no such thing as moral credit. And although we think we can, the forgiveness of sins (debts) cannot be purchased by good works—to suggest such an idea would be to add the sin of self-righteousness. Only God can cancel our moral debt.

Debts. Even someone who goes bankrupt tries to get going again. They don't just go deeper and deeper into debt. At least, they shouldn't! That would be downright criminal. Compare that bankruptcy to the loss of moral purity. Just because you're no longer as pure as the driven snow doesn't mean you should let your life become slush. But just the same, we can still be forgiven. In Luke 7:36–50, Luke has Jesus tell a Pharisee a parable about two debtors. A Pharisee had invited Him to dinner and complained when he saw a sinful woman anoint Jesus's feet with her tears and with oil, wiping them with her hair. One of the debtors in Jesus's story owed five hundred Denarii, and the other owed fifty. "When they could not pay, their creditor forgave them both. "Now, which of them will love him more?" The answer the host gave was well judged—it was the one who was forgiven most. Then Jesus said, "Therefore, I tell you, her sins, which are many, are forgiven, for she loved much; but he who is forgiven little loves little" (Luke 7:47).

Love merits Christ's forgiveness. Not status. Not intelligence. Not even good intentions or good works. But love. Love heals the wounds we open by sin. But the wound can still leave a scar. And a scar never fades completely. The consequences of our sins do not get erased. Our sins are never completely forgotten, (except by God!), not in this life, but the debt becomes paid. We can start out anew. We get a second chance. We must always remember that we have been hurt by sin. The pain may fade with the past. We may no longer feel it, but we still need to be morally sensitive. Forget the pain, but remember what caused the injury, and don't let it happen anymore. Love keeps no record of wrongs! (1 Corinthians 13:6). People who hold grudges either imagine the pain is still there, or they exaggerate the trauma brought on by the wound. They fail to move forward to start out anew, to start over. They live in the past, pointing at times when the wrong thing was done … however long ago it happened. Maybe that proves they were right, but they were right in the past, not the present, and pointing that out serves only themselves; it does not serve God or others. It shows no love. It serves no will but their own. Meanwhile, God's will must be done … today!

And God's will is that we forgive others, too! That will be the issue in the next chapter!

Scriptures

To discover more about what the Bible says about prayer and forgiveness, here are some scripture passages that will help to inspire us:

If my people who are called by my name humble themselves, pray, seek my face, and turn from their wicked ways, then I will hear from heaven, and will forgive their sin and heal their land. (2 Chronicles 7:14)

Do not repay evil for evil, but take thought for what is noble in the sight of all. (Romans 12:17)

Blessed are the merciful, for they shall receive mercy. (Matthew 5:7)

If another disciple sins, you must rebuke the offender, and if there is repentance, you must forgive. (Luke 17:3b)

All the prophets testify about him that everyone who believes in him receives forgiveness of sins through his name. (Acts 10:43)

But if anyone does sin, we have an advocate with the Father, Jesus Christ the righteous; and he is the atoning sacrifice for our sins, and not for ours only but also for the sins of the whole world. (1 John 2:1b-2)

Love covers a multitude of sins. (1 Peter 4:8b)

For I will be merciful toward their iniquities, and I will remember their sins no more. (Hebrews 8:12)

I, I am he who blots out your transgressions for my own sake, and I will not remember your sins. (Isaiah 43:25)

Indeed, God did not send the Son into the world to condemn the world, but in order that the world might be saved through him. (John 3:17)

Then Peter came and said to him, "Lord, if another member of the church sins against me, how often should I forgive? As many as seven times?" Jesus said to him, "Not seven times, but, I tell you, seventy-seven times." (Matthew 18:21–22)

He has rescued us from the power of darkness and transferred us into the kingdom of his beloved Son, in whom we have redemption, the forgiveness of sins. (Colossians 1:13–14)

Put away from you all bitterness and wrath and anger and wrangling and slander, together with all malice, and be kind to one another, tenderhearted, forgiving one another as God in Christ has forgiven you. (Ephesians 4:31)

What to Do

Share your needs.

Think about who can help you. Who can you help?

Think: How have you become a better person over the years? How have you improved? How are you growing?

Think: How have you been given second chances, (or third, or, fourth, … chances)?

Consider some of the things for which you have been forgiven. What have others done that you have forgiven?

Consider some of the ways you have been in debt. Consider some of the ways another may be indebted to you.

Be forgiving!

Remember that forgiveness is connected to repentance. How do you need to repent?

A Prayer

Almighty God, in Jesus Christ You take away the sins of the world. He died to do so. I believe in His gracious act on my behalf. He died in my place. Though I deserve to be punished, His mercy has set me free. Help me to never take for granted this wonderful blessing. Let me see myself as having cast off my worldly rags and put on the heavenly clothes that You have given me. I ask this prayer in Jesus's Name. Amen.

A Poem

I Will Keep Running
Whenever I think about all my mistakes,
I can't help but imagine the way God's heart breaks.
But God loves me so much that He sent me His Son
To take on my guilt for the evil I've done.
And though I accept this, I still seem to stray,
And I stumble and fail. I keep losing my way.
It's a wonderful gift—to know I'm forgiven
And raised to the light of God's kingdom of heaven.
I'm new in His mercy. I'm free from my past.
I'm hopeful. I'm happy. I'm learning at last
That though life is hard, I can still rise above
The struggles I'm facing with God's perfect love.

God isn't finished with me and my flaws,
But I will keep running this race without pause.

Chapter 5

AS WE FORGIVE

> … but if you do not forgive others,
> neither will your Father forgive your trespasses.
> —Matthew 6:15

The Church in Prayer

Every church, every religion, has some form of prayer. It is often something that is done corporately, as a community. Praying together can do something for us. It's not just a matter of everyone praying at the same time or praying their own prayers. As I said in the last chapter, it can be a matter of aligning our wills. Corporate prayer becomes more than the sharing of needs. It is taking those needs to heart and lifting them up together before God. When everyone is lifting something different, that's good, but it is hard to focus. Korean Christians have a method of prayer where everyone prays aloud at the same time. It sounds like chaos, but it's also quite inspiring. But if we all focused on what one person was lifting, as if we were all holding it up at the same time, perhaps that one thing would be something on which to concentrate. Think of a chant. If everyone were saying, "Go, Tom, go!" loudly and joyfully to encourage Tom, Tom would feel pretty encouraged! Inspired! But if some in the crowd were shouting "Go home, Tom," Tom might get a mixed message and become confused.

This is not to say that God can be confused. The point I want to make is that when there is unity concerning a certain need, an alignment of wills making a comtion appeal before God, it would seem to have more power. If everyone had a flashlight, and everyone was aiming it at the same object, that object would be easier to see—it would be much clearer. Prayer can be like that. We can be like that. We can be one body, one mind, one heart, desiring the things that God desires.

When we see football games, there are often cheerleaders. They get the crowds worked up to call on the team to do their best. It's similar when we are all praying the same prayers. Whether they are memorized or printed in a bulletin, they rally us around their words. Some don't like printed prayers because they don't think they are as inspired as spontaneous prayers. But the one who has originally written the prayer was inspired.

I have done hundreds of children's sermons. The kids in the worship service gather with me at the steps before the chancel area, and I usually have an object lesson. One time, I included the choir sitting nearby. I asked them all to sing their favorite hymns, and I had them all begin on the count of three. When they all began to sing, none of their voices made any sense. It was confusing and nonsense for the kids. Then I asked them all to sing the doxology together. It was beautiful, harmonious, and very understandable. When we are together for the sake of the words, it can be glorious.

Give Us This Day

The Lord's Prayer is a spotlight. It helps us all know what Jesus wants us to say to God. It helps us know what we need and what we should do. The Lord's Prayer gives us focus. It gives us a sense of our purpose. And our purpose is God's kingdom; and God's kingdom is holy, righteous, divine. God wants His children to be with Him in heaven. But we are not holy, nor righteous, nor divine. We need something to make us holy. Forgiveness makes that difference. Forgiveness is sometimes described as having our sins washed away. But if my sins have been washed away, and I have some brothers and sisters whose sins have not been washed away, I should want, and God wants, them to receive the same forgiveness that I have received. I can be the one who turns on the water, who gets my brother or sister into the shower. Faith is the soap, and God is the water tower and the source of the water. We all need a shower ... a spiritual shower. I don't really think we need to bathe together, though.

As We Forgive—It is God's will that we be reconciled to Him, that we be forgiven of our errors, that we return from straying, and that we seek the kingdom of heaven. It is also God's will that we be reconciled with our brothers and sisters—the others who might be able to pray: *Our Father.* After Peter asked Jesus how often he had to forgive his sinful brother, and Jesus told him not just seven times but seven times seventy times (Matthew 18:22 alternate reading), Jesus told a parable about forgiveness comparing the kingdom of heaven to a "king who wished to settle accounts with his servants" (Matthew 18:23–35). One servant, who owed the king ten thousand talents, begged for time, and the king had mercy. Then the servant went to one of his fellow servants who owed him one hundred denarii, demanding to be paid. He too begged for time but was given none. The creditor servant put him in jail, "Then his lord summoned him and said to him, 'You wicked servant! I forgave you all that debt because you besought me; and should you not have had mercy on your fellow servant as I had mercy on you?' And in anger, his lord delivered him to the jailors." Then Jesus says, "So also my heavenly Father will do to every one of you if you do not forgive your brother from your heart" (Matthew 18:35).

"If you forgive others their trespasses, your heavenly Father will also forgive you; but if you do not forgive others, neither will your Father forgive your trespasses!" (Matthew 6:14–15).

In a way, this petition of the Lord's Prayer is about being given the ability to forgive others. For it is *as we forgive others* that God will forgive us. Measure for measure. It is as we do unto others that God will do unto us. If we hold anything against another, God will hold it against us. If we do not do unto others what we would have others do unto us, and especially if we do not to unto others as we would hope God would do unto us, we are not doing the will of God!

Sometimes, we are so aware of the sins of others that we forget our own. "Why do you see the speck that is in your brother's eye, but do not notice the log that is in your own?" (Matthew 7:3). The artist DaVinci, who painted an enemy's face for the face of Judas, the betrayer of Christ, became unable to paint a face of Christ. He then felt guilty in holding that grudge and in expressing it so boldly. He finally painted his own face as Judas, and then, Christ became envisioned.

Sometimes, we get so vengeful that we forget our own need to be penitent. We imagine that God has a ledger of debts with everyone's name in it but our own. But that book was tossed out long ago. To keep a behavior ledger of any sort is wrong. There was an experience in Corinth that Paul addressed with grace and wisdom. It is assumed that someone had bad-mouthed Paul.

> "If anyone has caused pain, they have caused it not to me, but to some extent—not to exaggerate it—to all of you. This punishment by the majority is enough for such a person; so now instead you should forgive and console him, so that he may not be overwhelmed by excessive sorrow. So I urge you to reaffirm your love for this person. I wrote this for a reason: to test you and to know whether you are obedient in everything. Anyone whom you forgive, I also forgive. What I have forgiven, if I have forgiven anything, has been for your sake in the presence of Christ. And we do this to keep Satan from gaining an advantage over us; for we are not ignorant of his designs." (2 Corinthians 2:5–11)

With Paul, we must keep Satan from "gaining the advantage over us." With Paul, we should forgive and comfort the sinner rather than pour salt into his or her wounds.

Forgiveness has two dimensions: for *our* trespasses and for *those* who trespass against us. The Lord's Prayer hopes for God's will to be done … on earth as it is in heaven. And there is a need for a bridge between earth and heaven. The bridge is forgiveness. God is ready to forgive, but, in some ways, we are not always ready to be forgiven. An unforgiving spirit shuts the door on God's forgiveness for us. But this petition breaks the cycle of hate and anger, of vengeance and spite. Forgiveness is offered. We have been relieved of our debts. Now we must live as though it were true, giving to others what we know God has given to us.

A condition seems to be placed on the issue of forgiveness. If we want forgiveness, we must be forgiving! If we are not forgiving, we will not be forgiven!

And God has given us His promise, and His promise is a whole new relationship: "I will put my Law within them, and I will write it upon their hearts; and I will be their God and they shall be my people. And no longer shall each man teach his neighbor and each his brother, saying, 'Know the Lord!' for they shall all know me, from the least of them to the greatest, says the Lord; for I will forgive their iniquity, and I will remember their sin no more" (Jeremiah 31:33b-34).

And the promise, this new covenant, is something we celebrate in Communion. For it is a covenant of forgiveness, and the relationship we share includes reconciliation. "The old has passed away, behold, the new has come. All this is from God who through Christ gave us the ministry of reconciliation ... So we are ambassadors for Christ, God making His appeal through us, We beseech you on behalf of Christ, be reconciled to God. For our sake, He made Him to be sin who knew no sin, so that in Him we might become the righteousness of God" (2 Corinthians 5:17–21).

In Him. As Christ said: "Condemn not, and you will not be condemned" (Luke 6:37b KJV). Know, you will be raised in eternity, "Forgive, and you will be forgiven" (v. 37c). Yes, you will be washed clean of unrighteousness. "For the measure you give will be the measure you get back" (v. 38c). In Christ is life. If we are "in Him," we are ambassadors for Him, "God making His appeal through us" (2 Corinthians 5:20b).

Through us. O God, let forgiveness be known that the whole world may be reconciled to God. As we forgive those who trespass against us, forgive us too.

Scriptures

To discover more about what the Bible says about prayer and mercy, here are some scripture passages that will help to inspire us:

> The Lord, the Lord, a God merciful and gracious, slow to anger, and abounding in steadfast love and faithfulness, keeping steadfast love for the thousandth generation, forgiving iniquity and transgression and sin. (Exodus 34:6–7)

Know therefore that the Lord your God is God, the faithful God who maintains covenant loyalty with those who love him and keep his commandments, to a thousand generations. (Deuteronomy 7:9)

All the paths of the Lord are steadfast love and faithfulness, for those who keep his covenant and his decrees. (Psalm 25:10)

But you, O Lord, are a God merciful and gracious, slow to anger and abounding in steadfast love and faithfulness. (Psalm 86:15)

The Lord is gracious and merciful, slow to anger and abounding in steadfast love. The Lord is good to all, and his compassion is over all that he has made. (Psalm 145:8–9)

The steadfast love of the Lord never ceases, his mercies never come to an end; they are new every morning; great is your faithfulness. (Lamentations 3:22–23)

God, who is rich in mercy, out of the great love with which he loved us even when we were dead through our trespasses, made us alive together with Christ—by grace you have been saved—and raised us up with him and seated us with him in the heavenly places in Christ Jesus, so that in the ages to come he might show the immeasurable riches of his grace in kindness toward us in Christ Jesus. (Ephesians 2:4–7)

Let us therefore approach the throne of grace with boldness, so that we may receive mercy and find grace to help in time of need. (Hebrews 4:16)

Do not let loyalty and faithfulness forsake you; bind them around your neck, write them on the tablet of your heart. So you will find favor and good repute in the sight of God and of people. (Proverbs 3:3–4)

Those who are kind to the needy honor God. (Proverbs 14:31b)

Love mercy. (Micah 6:8)

Woe to you, scribes and Pharisees, hypocrites! For you tithe mint, dill, and cumin, and have neglected the weightier matters of the law: justice and mercy and faith. (Matthew 23:23)

Bear one another's burdens, and in this way you will fulfill the law of Christ. (Galatians 6:2)

As God's chosen ones, holy and beloved, clothe yourselves with compassion, kindness, humility, meekness, and patience. Bear with one another and, if anyone has a complaint against another, forgive each other; just as the Lord has forgiven you, so you also must forgive. (Colossians 3:12–14)

For judgment will be without mercy to anyone who has shown no mercy; mercy triumphs over judgment. (James 2:13)

Go and learn what this means, "I desire mercy, not sacrifice. For I have come to call not the righteous but sinners." (Matthew 9:13)

But you, beloved, build yourselves up on your most holy faith; pray in the Holy Spirit; keep yourselves in the love of God; look forward to the mercy of our Lord Jesus Christ that leads to eternal life. And have mercy on some who are wavering, save others by snatching them out of the fire; and have mercy on others with fear, hating even the tunic defiled by their bodies. (Jude 20–23)

But when the goodness and lovingkindness of God our Savior appeared, he saved us not because of any works of righteousness that we had done, but according to his mercy, through the water of rebirth and renewal by the Holy Spirit. (Titus 3:4–5)

Blessed be the God and Father of our Lord Jesus Christ! By his great mercy he has given us new birth into a living hope through the resurrection of Jesus Christ from the dead. (1 Peter 1:3)

What to Do

Think about the issues on which we could all focus the beams of our flashlights. What things would you like us all to see more clearly?

Consider being a sort of "cheerleader" for a cause. What cause is it?

Consider the ways your sins have been washed away. Who do you know that needs a shower?

Consider: How hard is it for you to be forgiving? ... to be merciful?

Consider: What grudges are you holding? Can you forgive that person? Can you love them?

Consider: How can holding a grudge give Satan an advantage?

Consider: How is forgiveness a bridge? ... between you and another? ... between earth and heaven?

Be an ambassador for Christ.

A Prayer

Almighty God, You are merciful and gracious, and You forgive my sins and transgressions. You relieve my debts. Help me to realize that in You I am rich enough to help others with their debts. Help me to enrich others by sharing Your forgiveness. Make me merciful, and I know I will be blessed with mercy. This I pray in Jesus's Name. Amen.

A Song

Manna in the Wilderness

We were hungry. We were full of fear.
We were in a barren land.
But when we cried out to our God
He raised a mighty hand.
Our brothers', sisters', fathers', mothers'
Graves were back in Egypt. Many souls had died.
Many friends and loved ones suffered.
Many simply bowed their heads and cried.

Manna in the wilderness—
Water from the rock—
God opens up the door of grace
Before we even knock.

Mercy came to raise us up
To carry us on eagles' wings;
Delivering us and saving us—
It gave us cause to sing!

Manna in the wilderness—
Water from the rock—
God opens up the door of grace
Before we even knock.

God made for us a pathway forward
Through waters by His power,
And He led us with His holy fire
Every day and every hour.

Manna in the wilderness—
Water from the rock—
God opens up the door of grace
Before we even knock.

Chapter 6

LEAD US NOT INTO TEMPTATION, BUT DELIVER US FROM EVIL

Blessed is anyone who endures temptation.
Such a one has stood the test and
will receive the crown of life
that the Lord has promised to those who love him.
No one, when tempted, should say, "I am being tempted by God";
for God cannot be tempted by evil and he himself tempts no one.
But one is tempted by one's own desire,
being lured and enticed by it;
then, when that desire has conceived, it gives birth to sin,
and sin, when it is fully grown, gives birth to death.
—James 1:12–15

The Act of Prayer—For the past five chapters, I have been sharing a few words at their beginning about the phenomenon of prayer. Prayer is an outward act of communication and an inner act of communion; It is an external act of encounter and an inner state of penetration. Prayer is an outward expression of an inward state of being. I would call prayer *the poetry of the soul*. But more than anything else, prayer is what makes us, as humans, the image and likeness of God.

True prayer is created by an attitude. E. Stanley Jones has said that "prayer is not so much an act as an attitude." And as I would repeat, it is an outward expression of an inward state of being, an inward attitude. The outward expression becomes *the act of prayer.* As a human activity, prayer is grounded in our faith. Prayer is not unique to any one religion. I believe it is the one phenomenon that is common to all forms of faith and belief, and I believe that everyone, whether they admit it or not, is prayerful at times, in one way or another. Have you ever talked to yourself?

Prayer can be done both in response and in need. We respond to life in our own way, and we all have unfulfilled needs. It is in the Christian faith, however, that I believe the sincerest response is taught, and the truest needs of humanity are made known and brought before God. And I believe that Christian prayer produces the attitude that is most closely aligned with the will of God for God's creation. That is why Christians should practice prayer. And for that reason, when people become members of the United Methodist Church, they vow to be loyal to the church by, among other things, their prayers.

As an act, prayer should be seen as deliberately coming before God and making requests. I have envisioned the act of prayer as a matter of stepping into the throne room of God, our King; articulating with respect our adoration, our confessions, our thanksgivings, and our supplications—the needs we want to lift. An easy acronym for remembering the process of prayer is ACTS. Prayers of supplication include our prayers for ourselves and our petitions on behalf of others. But, as I like to say, prayer is often a matter of "descending with the mind into the heart" (Theophan the Recluse).

When we pray, we use our minds; but our tears and our groans, our joy and our praise can all be expressed without having to do much thinking. Either way, as I have said, prayer is an act of presenting ourselves before the presence of God.

Give Us This Day

The purpose of prayer, for the Christian, is Christian living. And the purpose of Christian living is taken from the simple prayer that we've been studying in this book. This is the prayer that Jesus taught to His disciples.

In the Lord's Prayer, we repeatedly acknowledge this purpose, and yet, we too often take it for granted. The purpose is implicit in the words, "*Thy kingdom come ...*" The kingdom is the institution of God's love and reconciling forgiveness. And the way to fulfill this purpose is by fulfilling the petition: "*Thy will be done.*" We can do God's will by being loving and by caring for the will of God in and for God's world. And prayer is an act of aligning our wills as closely as possible to God's will. To do so is to be devoted to that will in a serious way.

And in whatever way we pray, we are being devotional beings. We take on an attitude that acknowledges God's presence in our lives. If we ever felt that we had no need to pray because we were self-sufficient, we would only be fooling ourselves. We can, at times, be so satisfied with our own lives that we feel no need to pray. If so, what are we doing for the kingdom? For others? Are we not aware of the needs of others? I have taught people that if they want to know what to pray about, read the news. The world is rife with desperate needs.

And if we ever feel that our prayers are left unanswered, we should remember that no is an answer too. We may be praying for a wrong reason, or for something that we don't really need, something that wouldn't ever serve to advance the kingdom. Paul prayed for his "thorn in the flesh" to be removed. God didn't remove it, and God gave Paul the message that "My grace is sufficient for you, for my power is made perfect in weakness" (2 Corinthians 12:9). We must remember that prayer is for the sake of the kingdom and that we pray in the Spirit for the needs of our souls and for every aspect of life throughout the world. We pray for God's kingdom to manifest itself in the world.

Another answer to our prayers can also be "wait."

Sometimes, prayer can be described as a kind of light. As our light shines, it may not always give *us* any more illumination, but, like a beacon, it can give light for someone else who may need it. Or, like a flashlight, prayer might not help us here, where the lamp is held, and we might not even see the direction of the beam, but that light might be shining somewhere where we don't notice, cutting through a darkness we could not feel. It shines here, and it reflects there, but how prayer gets from here to there might be difficult for us to see.

But prayer becomes a beacon, a guiding light, that leads us safely onward. And as the lighthouse leads the ships *away* from the dangerous rocks and guides them safely into the harbor, so also do we, in the house of God, pray, *lead us not into temptation, but deliver us from evil.*

Lead Us—Our Lord's Prayer includes the petition for God to lead us, for God's Word to be our guide, for the Way of Christ to be our way—the Way, the Truth, and the Life (John 14:6). Three dimensions of guidance are invoked by the idea of being led. First, it includes receiving directions—where to go and what road or pathway to take. Any person can lead us in this way if they have been there before. Second, it includes the idea of going before, for others to follow. Following someone's lead. This includes the purpose of the leader. Much like a shepherd, God's leadership is dependable and secure. Consider Psalm 23:1, 2b—"The Lord is my shepherd … He leads me beside still waters." Sheep have a terrible fear of flowing water. Just as it is hard for us to swim with our clothes and shoes on, imagine how much harder it would be for a sheep, with their little feet, whose wool became saturated with water were it to fall off the bank while taking a drink. In biblical times, the shepherd would use the rocks by the bank of a creek to form a small pool where his sheep could come to drink. And the rod, or staff, of the shepherd would always be close by. Feeling it there, the sheep would know they were protected. "Thy rod and thy staff, they comfort me" (Psalm 23:4d). God, like the shepherd, "Leads us in the paths of righteousness … even though I walk through the valley of the shadow of death, I fear no evil, for Thou art with me" (23:3b-4). God is leading me, protecting me, guiding me to greener pastures. The Lord is my shepherd. I want nothing more. And Jesus Christ is the Good Shepherd! (John 10:11).

The Hebrews, freed from the yoke of Pharaoh, were led safely by God, not by "way of the land of the Philistines" (Exodus 13:17), the shortest way, for that would lead them into conflict and war. They were safer in the wilderness. And God "went before them … by day in a pillar of cloud, and by night in a pillar of fire" (Exodus 13:21). God led the children of Israel away from the temptation of war, the way the lighthouse beacon leads the ship away from the dangerous rocks.

A third dimension of being led is into the future, not from the past only, but from the present as well. This includes having goals to guide us and promises to fulfill. We live by the standards of a heavenly promise, something not yet but determined to be—Thy kingdom come! The promise of salvation is for believers and followers of Christ. But salvation is now; it is our pilot and our destination. It is the course and the winds that fill our sails. Christ has gone before us, but Christ is here beside us, within us by His Spirit. Christ compels us.

Lead Us—One other aspect of God's leadership is the fact of the call. There is a calling we hear, a word that comes to us that beckons us. And we are meant to respond. For some, the call is inward and compelling. For others, the call is from an external source and inspiring. But that call—that voice of truth—is leading us in our faith journeys.

Lead Us Not into Temptation—Lead us *not* into temptation. Give us endurance, keep us on course, don't let us give in to the tug of evil. What are our temptations? What is it that draws us off course? Something that tempts us lures us. It lures us away from faith and pulls us into the occasion for sin. Christ was tempted (Matthew 4:3–11; Luke 4:5–13). The first two temptations were to use supernatural powers: to use His own power to turn stones into bread to satisfy his physical hunger, and the power of God to keep Him from falling. The third temptation was to submit to the power of evil and to worship Satan.

The use of personal abilities for personal gain is something we're all tempted to do. How often do we throw our weight around just to seem as though we had control or to prove we had some control? We do it to fulfill ego needs. But Christ had a real hunger, and rather than expressing His faith as faith in Himself, He depended on His faith in God. Nothing was going to pull Him away from God and dare Him to minister only to Himself. Because of His faith, when the devil left Him, "angels came and ministered to Him" (Matthew 4:11). We should never think it right to serve only ourselves. What we serve is God's kingdom!

The temptation to use our faith in frivolous demonstrations of divine presence in our lives is also something to avoid. Christ, standing on the pinnacle of the temple in Jerusalem, was told, "Prove that you are the Son

of God! Throw yourself down; angels will catch you; they won't let you fall."
Sometimes, people use the wonderful gifts they have to show that God is
with them, rather than to show that they are with God. The temptation is
to be proud—proud that we know Christ, proud that we feel saved, proud
that our sins have been forgiven. We are cleansed of all sin … all but the
sin of pride, when we succumb to the temptation to boast of what God has
done for us, rather than speak with the spirit of a humble servant. Christ
would let nothing influence the course of His mission to seek and to save
the lost. What influences the course of our mission as Christians?

In the final temptation, which is both a lure toward power and an
occasion for idolatry, Satan uses every ounce of ammo he's got: "All the
kingdoms of the world if you only worship me" (Matthew 4:9). But the
kingdoms of this world were not Satan's to give! Satan is a liar! And Christ's
answer is simply, "Be gone!" Christ could not be swayed—"You shall
worship the Lord your God, and Him only shall you serve!" (Matthew
4:10). Him only. What makes us forget God? I would wager that God is
usually forgotten when we put ourselves first, before His kingdom, when
we become self-serving. We want the kingdom to serve us rather than for
us to serve the kingdom.

Temptations are sometimes tests of faith, stumbling blocks to service,
and trials to weaken us. Note, however, that even Jesus was tempted. It is
not a sin to be tempted. It is sinful to give in to temptation! Remember
what James said: "One is tempted by one's own desire, being lured and
enticed by it; then when that desire has conceived, it gives birth to sin, and
that sin, when it is fully grown, gives birth to death" (1:14–15). To ask God
to lead us *not* into temptation is to pray for escape and endurance. Unless a
ship can ride out the storm, it wasn't fit to sail. We court temptation rather
than tend our moorings and secure what holds us together. What makes
us endure? By enduring, we can prove our faith and the power of God
working in us and through us. Too often we feel like giving up, and we
make excuses for ourselves. *Lead us not into temptation*: prove our loyalty,
confirm our conviction, maintain our commitment. Deliver us from our
inner conflicts and our outward lures. Deliver us, O God, deliver us!

Deliver Us from Evil—The whole theme of the Bible is that of
deliverance. We pray that we will be delivered not only from the constant

lures that take us away from what is good, but from those evils that try our faith—those pains and frustrations, those accidents and errors that push us over the brink. We pray these words because we can't deliver ourselves! We are weak when it comes to such agonizing perplexities that we are tempted to say, "Why me, God?" or, "God, where are You?" And where *is* God when the hurricane hits, or when a child is kidnapped, abused, and killed? Where is God? We are tempted to think that God is not in control, and maybe evil is. Deliver us, O Lord. Deliver us. To pray this says we claim that God *is* in control. God holds us; we don't hold God. The reason evil's destruction and maliciousness still occurs is that even though God's kingdom is among us, it is nowhere near complete. We still live in a fallen world. Besides, we haven't been the builders that we're meant and commissioned to be. When God's will is done completely, God's kingdom will come completely. O God, deliver us!

Deliver—The Post Office delivers. Moses delivered the Hebrews out of Egypt. Deliver means hand over, as in the mail; it means give forth, as with a sermon; liberate; release; save; redeem. But it is always in a sense of coming *from* something else, as in being delivered *from* evil. But there is a way of understanding the word *deliver* that I believe we need to acknowledge. Babies are delivered at their birth. Such a delivery is into life, into a new world. We are not delivered from anything evil when we are born, but that deliverance makes us fully alive. When we are born anew, we are delivered into a spiritual world, a world of faith, a world where we become aware of good and evil and aware of what to pursue and what to avoid. To pray for this deliverance is to pray for this birth, this new life to ignite within us and burn with love and hope for the kingdom to come and for God's will to be done!

From Evil—Deliver us from *evil*. It is possible to translate this petition as saying, "Deliver us from *the evil one*." But that limits the meaning of the prayer to an evil in particular, whereas I believe it should encompass all wrongs and injustices. Evil can be moral, or it can be spiritual. When it is moral, it is emotionally painful as well as injurious and troublesome. When it is spiritual, it is malicious, perverse, and wicked, having to do with intentions that are not to the benefit of God's kingdom. There is a fine line between moral and spiritual evil, but both hurt, both need correction, and both give witness to corruption and sin.

Old Testament theology saw the presence of evil as a punishment for sin. If that were entirely true, what sin did Adam and Eve commit when they came into the presence of the serpent? The serpent just happened to be present! I don't believe it was a part of God's plan that we suffer evil; suffering is a part of mortal existence though. Out of our struggles, we can grow. But suffering is a consequence of our limitations, our weaknesses, and our fallenness; and it should prove to us how much we need one another to make it through. Perhaps God's plan might include the allowance of things we might consider evil, but only insofar as it evokes in us the understanding that we need to help one another, and we need to live *by* faith *in* dependence on God. We need to live as though we were living for God not for ourselves because to live for God would result in serving others. These last two petitions of the Lord's Prayer are asking God to *lead us* and *deliver us*. It's not about myself as an individual but about all who might call God Father!

When I was in seminary, one professor sent us on a "treasure hunt." The only stipulation was that we all had to stay together, all twenty-four of us. I can tell you now that the treasure we found was nothing like the treasure we expected. The first clue was "the phone booth at the end of the parking lot." (There were phone booths back then, 1978) A note there, read after all of us arrived and were together, said, "One half of you has just become lame." The next clue was to go to the bell tower. We paired up, and one person in each pair had to act as though he or she had a wounded leg, and those of us who were still uninjured became their servants, helping them continue. Needless to say, we moved much more slowly. At the bell tower, the note said, "The other half just became blind; go back to the classroom." Suddenly, with the help of many blindfolds, we were all the blind leading the lame. I was blind. Somehow, now, we had to listen to the guidance of our partners, as we helped them walk. We were serving each other, trusting each other, helping each other.

In a way, it was as if a miracle happened. When we finally returned to the classroom, the professor said, "You have all just experienced the kingdom of God." You see, we all had to lead each other away from stumbling blocks, and we all had to deliver each other from the evils of our disabilities. We may have moved more slowly, but, still, we moved. And God moved within us all.

We are the blind leading the lame. God is our light, and God is our shepherd. But God can work in us, even though we are suffering from evil of some kind, and, for each other, we can be light, and we can be shepherds.

Scriptures

To discover more about what the Bible says about prayer and temptation, here are some scripture passages that will help to inspire us:

Pray, lest ye enter into temptation. (Luke 22:46b KJV)

God is faithful, and he will not let you be tested beyond your strength, but with the testing he will also provide the way out so that you may be able to endure the testing. (1 Corinthians 10:13)

For anyone who lacks these things is short-sighted and blind, and is forgetful of the cleansing of past sins. (2 Peter 1:9)

But those who want to be rich fall into temptation and are trapped by many senseless and harmful desires that plunge people into ruin and destruction. (1 Timothy 6:9)

Blessed is anyone who endures temptation. Such a one has stood the test and will receive the crown of life that the Lord has promised to those who love him. (James 1:12)

Can fire be carried in the bosom without burning one's clothes? Can one walk on hot coals without scorching the feet? (Proverbs 6:27–28)

You know that the testing of your faith produces endurance. (James 1:3)

My friends, if anyone is detected in a transgression, you who have received the Spirit should restore such a one in a spirit of gentleness. (Galatians 6:1)

For we do not have a high priest who is unable to sympathize with our weaknesses, but we have one who in every respect has been tested as we are, yet without sin. (Hebrews 4:15)

Therefore take up the whole armor of God, so that you may be able to withstand on that evil day, and having done everything, to stand firm. (Ephesians 6:13)

For you, O God, have tested us; you have tried us as silver is tried. (Psalm 66:10)

Do not be overcome by evil, but overcome evil with good. (Romans 12:21)

Discipline yourselves. Keep alert. Like a roaring lion your adversary the devil prowls around, looking for someone to devour. (1 Peter 5:8)

Be angry but do not sin; do not let the sun go down on your anger, and do not make room for the devil. (Ephesians 4:26–27)

Put to death, therefore, whatever in you is earthly: fornication, impurity, passion evil desire and greed (which is idolatry). (Colossians 3:5)

For the grace of God has appeared, bringing salvation to all, training us to renounce impiety and worldly passions, and in the present age to live lives that are self-controlled, upright and godly, while we wait for the blessed hope and manifestation of the glory of our great God and savior, Jesus Christ. (Titus 2:11–12)

What to Do

Resist evil.

Be alert. The devil is out there!

Consider: How are temptations like tests?

Be heavenly-minded, not worldly-minded.

Consider: How is prayer like "descending with the mind into the heart"?

Consider: How is prayer like putting on "the armor of God"?

See prayer as an act of aligning our wills as closely as possible to God's will.

See prayer as a flashlight shining on a certain need. What if we all focused our lights on that need together?

Let God lead you. Get His directions, or follow Him, or let Him deliver you into new life.

Think about your goals. How do they lead you forward?

Consider: What are the influences in your life? How do they seem to lead you?

A Prayer

Almighty God, we pray to be delivered from evil, and yet we are not prepared against it. Help us to let You lead us, to help us. Immerse us in Your Word in such a way that we know Your will and can perform it. Give us grace to follow the example of Your Son, our Lord. And guide us by Your perfect light. In Jesus's Name I pray. Amen.

A Poem

Stumbling Blocks
The world is full of stumbling blocks.
    They lure us and entice us until they make us fall.
What we need are stepping-stones
    And courageous persistence somehow to endure it all

Within us there's a grace at work.
    It feeds us and it strengthens us and gives to us a power
To rise above temptation's pull
    And gain new victories every hour.

And when I falter, when I'm weak,
    I'll call on faith and patience to resist
Until I can rebuke the fear
    That cowers in the darkness of this horrid evil test.

    I am able to put up the fight
    And faithfully then do what is right.

Chapter 7

NOT MY WILL BUT THINE

Then Jesus went with them to a place called Gethsemane;
and he said to his disciples, "Sit here while I go over there and pray."
He took with him Peter and the two sons of Zebedee,
and began to be grieved and agitated.
Then he said to them, "I am deeply grieved, even to death;
remain here, and stay awake with me."
And going a little farther, he threw himself on the ground and prayed,
"My Father, if it is possible, let this cup pass from me;
yet not what I want but what you want."
Then he came to the disciples and found them sleeping;
and he said to Peter, "So, could you not stay awake with me one hour?
Stay awake and pray that you may not come into the time of trial;
the spirit indeed is willing, but the flesh is weak."
Again he went away for the second time and prayed,
"My Father, if this cannot pass unless I drink it, your will be done."
Again he came and found them sleeping for their eyes were heavy.
So leaving them again, he went away and prayed for the third time,
saying the same words.
Then he came to his disciples and said to them,
"Are you still sleeping and taking your rest?
See, the hour is at hand, and the Son of Man is
betrayed into the hands of sinners."
—Matthew 26:36–44

The anguish of our Lord was immense ... and growing. Jesus and eleven of His disciples had come to the Garden of Gethsemane. As He stepped aside from all but three, Matthew says that "He began to be sorrowful and troubled" (Matthew 26:37 New Living Translation). He was beginning to bear the burden of my sin, of your sin, of all sin. Into Him was being poured the poison of our guilt and the pain of our shame. Like a cup of poison, He had to swallow it all. "My soul is overwhelmed with sorrow ... to the point of death" (v. 38a New International Version). And so Jesus prayed.

The total weight of fallen human nature began to press in on Him. Everything unholy and unrighteous began to course through His system like a fever. Luke describes the distress as being so intense that Jesus began to perspire. "And His sweat was like drops of blood falling to the ground" (22:44). God is holy. Jesus is God. But God's holiness and human failure cannot exist together, so Jesus must have felt as though everything divine within Him was pulling back. Not pulling away but withdrawing into the unreachable recesses of His being. Imagine a sort of adrenalin rush in reverse. The flight instinct is receding as the sacrificial purpose is seething forward. And in His mind, Jesus is beginning to feel the forsakenness of what He must endure.

And so He prays. He prays for endurance. But His anguish is unbearable ... even for the One who is the Incarnation of God! And He begins to imagine that there must be some other way. "My Father, if it is possible, may this cup be taken from me!" (v. 39). He knows that with God all things are possible. But this was The Plan. Perhaps there was no other way for the world to understand the greatness of God's mercy and love. God wanted to let people know there was a way to overcome sin. God wanted to redeem us from our guilt. God wanted to remove our punishment. And the death of His Son was to be the atoning sacrifice!

Jesus was innocent, perfect, and yet He bore my guilt, our guilt. He took the punishment we all deserve. "God made Him to be sin who had no sin, so that in Him we might become the righteousness of God!!!" (2 Corinthians 5:21). And so He prayed ... "Not my will, but Thine be done" (Luke 22:42 New KJV).

It was a moment of great resolve ... and great resignation. In humility, Jesus not only agreed to His fate; He accepted it. He committed to it ... again and again. Jesus shows us the way of humility, of self-abnegation, of self-denial. He relinquished His will. He surrendered Himself. He resigned

Himself to the perfect will of God's great purpose for the creation He loves, for the lost He wants to find, for the spiritually dead He wants to give new life!

Christ had even said, "I have come down from heaven not to do my will but to do the will of Him who sent me. And this is the will of Him who sent me, that I lose none of all that He has given me, but raise them up at the Last Day! For my Father 's will is that everyone who looks to the Son and believes in Him shall have eternal life, and I will raise them up at the Last Day!" (John 6:38–40). Jesus came to do God's will. And to show us how.

And He taught us to pray: *Thy will be done*! Of course, God always does what God wills. What we are praying for when we pray the Lord's Prayer is that we, too, would always do what God wills. But the problem is that we have our own wills. We want to do what *we* want, and we, in our fallen state, can be selfish, self-willed, and self-centered. We do not do God's will automatically. But we can choose. We must choose.

Human free will is a difficult challenge for theologians. We think that since God is all-powerful, God can, and should, make us do His will. But if He did so, all the time, then we would not be free to choose. But we *are* free. Our freedom is a part of our likeness to God. We can choose to resist God's will. We can even choose the influences in our lives. Ask any teenager, who do you want to decide with, your parents or your friends? … your church or your culture? … religion or the world? There seem to be almost endless options and alternatives.

But faith can make all the difference. There is nothing that serves better in the prevention of sinful behavior than faith. We may learn that we can get away with doing almost anything when it comes to our parents, our teachers and preachers, our friends, or the law, but not with God. First, most people eventually get caught. The odds are pretty good for that. We learn that eventually what goes around comes around. But God always knows. God knows our hearts and minds, as well as our actions. But still God gives us free will. And God gives us a choice.

In the Garden of Gethsemane, Jesus made a choice. And each of us, as did Jesus, must decide: My will or God's will? Our choices may seem to have little to do with choosing to suffer. But the fact of the matter is that when we choose our own way rather than God's way, we will suffer. Sin has eternal consequences, if not immediate: suffering and hell. Righteousness has eternal consequences too: glory and heaven!

Our problem is that opportunities to choose never stop. But Paul advised: "I appeal to you, brothers and sisters, by the mercies of God, to present your bodies as a living sacrifice, holy and acceptable to God, which is your spiritual worship. Do not be conformed to this world, but be transformed by the renewing of your minds, so that you may discern what is the will of God what is good and acceptable and perfect!" (Romans 12: 1–2).

What a joy it is to do the will of God—to be so "in Christ" that we begin to walk in the way of God's will, naturally, constantly realizing and discovering what is good and acceptable and perfect. What a glorious life it is, this life of faith!

Jesus made Himself a living sacrifice. He let go so God could truly use Him. And we too, need to let go. We need to agree, to choose to do, not whatever we want to do, but what God wants. Not my will but Thine be done!

Say it for yourself: Not my will but Thine be done!

Think it often. And do so … in remembrance of Christ!

Scriptures

To discover more about what the Bible says about prayer and resignation, here are some scripture passages that will help to inspire us:

> O Lord, you are our Father; we are the clay, and you are our potter; we are all the work of your hand. (Isaiah 64:8)

> Naked I came from my mother's womb, and naked shall I return there; the Lord gave, and the Lord has taken away; blessed be the name of the Lord. (Job 1:21)

> Shall we receive the good at the hand of the Lord and not receive the bad? (Job 2:10b)

> Am I not to drink the cup that the Father has given me? (John 18:11)

So in the present case, I tell you, keep away from these men and let them alone; because if this plan or this undertaking is of human origin, it will fail; but if it is of God, you will not be able to overthrow them—in that case you may even be found fighting against God! (Acts 5:38–39)

For me living is Christ and dying is gain. (Philippians 1:20)

I know what it is to have little, and I know what it is to have plenty. In any and all circumstances I have learned the secret of being well-fed and of going hungry, of having plenty and of being in need. (Philippians 4:12)

I appeal to you therefore, brothers and sisters, by the mercies of God, to present your bodies as a living sacrifice, holy and acceptable to God, which is your spiritual worship. (Romans 12:1)

I am ready not only to be bound but even to die in Jerusalem for the name of the Lord Jesus. (Acts 21:13)

So we do not lose heart. Even though our outer nature is wasting away our inner nature is being renewed day by day. (2 Corinthians 4:16)

But who are you, a human being, to argue with God? Will what is molded say to the one who molds it, "Why have you made me like this?" Has the potter no right over the clay, to make out of the same lump an object for special use and another for ordinary use? (Romans 9:20–21)

I have been crucified with Christ; and it is no longer I who live, but Christ who lives in me. And the life I now live in the flesh I live by faith in the Son of God, who loved me and gave himself for me. (Galatians 2:19b–20)

Submit yourselves therefore to God. Resist the devil and he will flee from you. (James 4:7)

Humble yourselves before the Lord, and he will exalt you. (James 4:10)

"If any want to become my followers, let them deny themselves and take up their cross and follow me. For those who want to save their lives will lose it, and those who lose their life for my sake will find it. (Matthew 16:24–25)

Trust in the Lord with all your heart, and do not rely on your own insight. In all your ways acknowledge him and he will make straight your paths. (Proverbs 3:5–6)

Do nothing from selfish ambition or conceit, but in humility regard others as better than yourselves. Let each of you look not to your own interests, but to the interests of others. (Philippians 2:3–4)

What to Do

Relinquish your will to the will of God … completely.

Submit. Surrender. Sacrifice yourself.

Think about how Jesus felt taking on your sin, your shame, your guilt.

Think about these words from above: "Perhaps there was no other way for the world to understand the greatness of God's mercy and love." Could there be other ways?

Think: How hard is humility for you?

Think about these words from above: "We do not do God's will automatically. But we can choose. We must choose." Think of how hard (or easy) it is to make this choice.

Be transformed by the renewing of your mind.

Think of the potter—clay imagery. How are you being molded right now?

Deny yourself!

A Prayer

Almighty God, take *me* away and let Your Spirit live in me. Help me let go of control so that You might mold me into the vessel You want me to be. Let me never fear the change that might come should I completely surrender to Your Way. But give me such confidence in You that I can trust Your heavenly will for my life. This I pray in Jesus's Name. Amen.

A Poem

Surrender Is Not Easy
Surrender is not easy, Lord.
    There's too much to give away.
I'm used to being who I am,
    So I know I need to pray.
It's Your will that I want to do—
    Your way I hope to find—
It's not about me, Lord. It's all about You—
    Your thoughts within my mind.
Catch me, Lord, when I let go,
    And hold me in Your light.
All I really want to know
    Is that Your way is right.

    When I have prayed, "Thy will be done,"
    Then I will know the battle's won.

Chapter 8

KINGDOM, POWER, AND GLORY FOREVER, AMEN

After the sabbath, as the first day of the week was dawning,
Mary Magdalene and the other Mary went to see the tomb.
And suddenly there was a great earthquake;
for an angel of the Lord, descending from heaven,
came and rolled back the stone
and sat on it.
His appearance was like lightning, and his clothing white as snow.
For fear of him the guards shook and became like dead men.
But the angel said to the women,
"Do not be afraid;
I know that you are looking for Jesus who was crucified.
He is not here; for he has been raised, as he said.
Come, see the place where he lay.
Then go quickly and tell his disciples,
'He has been raised from the dead
and indeed he is going ahead of you to Galilee;
there you will see him.'
This is my message for you."
—Matthew 28:1–7

The Place of Prayer in Our Lives

After Bertel Thorvaldsen (1770–1844) had completed his famous statue of Christ, he brought a friend to see it. Christ's arms were outstretched, His head bowed between them. The friend criticized the work by saying that from wherever he stood he could not see the face of Christ. "Yes," said the sculptor, "if you would see the face of Christ, you must get down on your knees."

It seems that worshipping on our knees is one way of being humble before the divine presence of God. In prayer, I have said that in a way, we present ourselves to the presence of God. There is no perfect position and no perfect method to do so, but the suggestion offered by Thorvaldsen evokes the necessity of prayer, or, at least, humbling ourselves, to see Christ face-to-face.

I would only want to briefly urge that prayer could be a way of being with God in the world. We need it. Sometimes, it seems, we need it more and more each year as humanity propels itself deeper into the pace of technological velocity. Personally, prayer is the one thing that holds me more accountable to God's heavenly kingdom. It is for the sake of the kingdom that we pray, even when we pray for our own needs, because we too are children of the kingdom, and to best serve our Lord, we must have our needs met, both spiritually and physically. Though this is not a qualifier or a requirement for service. The kingdom is our destiny and our purpose. We seek it, and we serve it now. The place of prayer in anyone's life is important, for it, in some degree, determines the place of the soul in the kingdom of God. Without prayer, and the faithful attitude toward living, loving, and the personal enrichment of our relationship with God, others, as well as ourselves, we are more likely to be humanists than true Christians. The prayers we offer are the songs of the kingdom, the poetry of the soul.

Imagine a wheel with many spokes. Imagine that each spoke represents a life. The hub of the wheel, its center, is God. As each spoke gets closer to the center, it is also, naturally, getting closer to the other spokes. Faith and prayer do this. No one should think he or she can get closer to God without being willing to be closer to others. Prayer should never isolate us. I believe it should make us more and more aware of other souls like ourselves. Others have the same needs, the same hopes for themselves, and for the world. Perhaps for a time it might seem appropriate to cloister ourselves for the sake of learning, retreating from the world. But we are meant to be in relationships with others. As much as we might pursue a vertical posture, looking upward to the divine, we can never deny the horizontal circumstance of our lives. We are at this crossroads all the time.

Nonetheless, we rejoice in the glory of God's kingdom and power. Doing so is ... glorious!

Give Us This Day

Kingdom, Power, and Glory

And there is a *kingdom* that's known only by the heart. It has no beginning, no end, no castles, and no borders. There is no wall about it to keep anyone in or out. It is led to by no roads, but there is a Way; and it's approached by a journey. But the journey is not one of distance, for this kingdom is reached by a pilgrimage of faith. The kingdom is nowhere, yet it is everywhere. It is a kingdom not to be seen with the eye, but it can be felt in the soul. It cannot be displayed, but it can be experienced. It is a kingdom that does not conquer, and yet it draws all nations to its realm. Its conqueror was a victim; His kingdom is a kingdom of kindness, a kingdom of peace, a kingdom of salvation and of reconciliation; a kingdom of redemption and of freedom. It's a kingdom where all become equal, and yet all become servants; it's a kingdom of the spirit, and yet it still serves the flesh. It's a kingdom of goodness; it's a kingdom of love. And Christ is the King—His authority is proven by His glorious defeat of death! Thine is the kingdom, O God, Thine is the throne!

And a *power* is manifested by this kingdom. It does not destroy, but it does make things new, and it does make things change. It does not boast in victory, but it does issue praise. It is a power we can feel, and yet the power is not ours. It's a power we hold, and yet it is not our own. It holds us as well. For the power is weakness and folly. It bears no worldly armor and wields no worldly weapon; it is seen in submission, and it's whispered in hope. Its force is its spending of itself. Its effect is its cause. For it's a power that draws from the efforts of its use. It comes from the source of our spirits, our souls, and it touches our flesh and inspires our minds. It teaches us to be still, and it compels us to move. It lays down our lives and it lifts us to great heights. It raises the dead, and it gives us new life. Thine is the power, O God, Thine is the might!

And there is a *glory* that is brought by this power. It's a glory that's humble, awarded no earthly crown. It comes as a treasure, and yet it's not countable. It's known in a victory that comes to the heart. It's a feeling of triumph, unboastingly silent; it is praise that is offered beyond what is visible. It is lifted in song, and it bows down our heads. This glory is given as a blessing for the hopeless, and yet it's a hope that builds trust in God's mercy. For it's a glory of death that brings life eternal. And Thine is the glory, O God, Thine is the praise!

Forever

And there is a time that we know of that never begins, yet it happens around us, within us, and through us without ceasing. We call it *forever* because it is now, and it feels eternal. It seems without end in days or in miles. And it carries on after we meet all our limits. Forever, eternity, fulfillment of time, another dimension beyond mortal thought. *Forever* is now, and forever is after. It comes from before; sometimes, it comes from tomorrow. But forever is always, world without end.

Amen

And the heart says *Amen* to words offered sincerely. It is as it's said when it's said as the truth. *So be it.* Thine is the kingdom and the Power and the Glory, forever. Amen!

The Lord's Prayer, in the sixth chapter of Matthew, seems so unfinished. And so a doxology attached through tradition is added when we pray its words to round it all out. The words are familiar as if taken from the prayer of David offered at the end of his life for the beginning of the building of the temple in Jerusalem. "Yours, O Lord, are the greatness, the power, the glory, and the majesty; for all that is in the heavens and on the earth is yours; yours is the kingdom, O Lord, and you are exalted as head above all" (1 Chronicles 29:11).

Thine is the kingdom. The emphasis is on God. The kingdom belongs to God. The kingdom is for us to enter, but it belongs to God. The bridge that opens the kingdom to us is determined for our crossing by the relationships we have. Human to human as well as human to divine, the bridge is built first, by doing God's will on earth; not by doing it as we choose but doing it as it is done in heaven. And second, the bridge is built by forgiveness: God forgives us our trespasses as we forgive those who have trespassed against us.

Thine is the power. The power of faith is not ours. Faith is not our power, but God's. And the way this power is shown is through love. And love is something that serves rather than provokes, as some forms of power seem to do. It encourages rather than persecutes. Love brings a growth rather than a limitation. Paul, himself, bears witness to the power of grace, for through Paul, God's power was made perfect in weakness (2 Corinthians 12:9). First Corinthians 2:1–5 says: "When I came to you, I did not come proclaiming to you the testimony of God in lofty words or wisdom. For I decided to know nothing among you except Jesus Christ and Him crucified. And I was with you in weakness and in much fear and trembling; and my speech and my message were not in plausible words of wisdom, but in demonstration of the Spirit of power, that your faith might rest not in the wisdom of mortals, but in the power of God." Faith is a divine power that is working through us.

In the New Testament, there are two words for "power." One is *exousia*, which is the force of authority; and the other is *dunamis*, from which the word dynamo or dynamite is derived. There were occasions when Christ bore witness to the dynamo of God's power within Himself, as He was able to heal and perform miracles and raise from the dead. And there were occasions when Christ had the authority to forgive sins, for example. In His final commission to His disciples in the Gospel of Matthew, the risen Jesus said, "All authority (exousia) in heaven and on earth has been given to me" (Matthew 28:18). And because of this, this power, the disciples were all the more able to compel people by their witness to become followers of Jesus. "And lo," because of this power, Christ said, "I am with you always" (28:20).

And Thine is the Glory! Toward the end of Jesus's public ministry, in the Gospel of John, Jesus found a young donkey and rode it into the city, and as He came near, the people who had witnessed His raising of Lazarus from the tomb and many others with them, took branches of palm trees and went out to meet Him crying: "Hosanna. Blessed is He who comes in the Name of the Lord, even the King of Israel" (John 12:13). After this, as it appeared that the whole world was beginning to know Jesus was the Christ, Jesus said, "The hour has come for the Son of Man to be glorified." And then He began to talk of His death: "Very truly, I tell you, unless a grain of wheat falls to the earth and dies, it remains just a single grain; but if it dies, it bears much fruit. Those who love their life lose it, and they who hate their life in this world will keep it for eternal life" (John 12:23–24). And rather than praying for God to save His life, he prays for God to glorify His Name—God's Name. And so God is glorified as His Son dies. And He died to live again, giving eternal life to all who would believe. And we believe in the Resurrection!

Thine is the kingdom and the Power and the Glory. Forever, eternally, without end either in time or in space, for the kingdom is for all people, and the power is for the love that it inspires.

Thine is the kingdom and the Power and the Glory … forever. Amen! Truly, amen!

Scriptures

To discover more about what the Bible says about prayer and glory, here are some scripture passages that will help to inspire us:

> Declare his glory among the nations, his marvelous works among all the peoples. (1 Chronicles 16:24)

> The heavens are telling the glory of God; and the firmament proclaims his handiwork. (Psalm 19:1)

> The earth is filled with the knowledge of the glory of the Lord, as the waters cover the sea. (Habakkuk 2:14)

And one called to another and said: "Holy, holy, holy is the Lord of hosts; the whole earth is full of his glory." (Isaiah 6:3)

Then your light shall break forth like the dawn, and your healing shall spring up quickly; your vindicator shall go before you, and the glory of the Lord shall be your rearguard. (Isaiah 58:8)

The Word became flesh and lived among us, and we have seen his glory, the glory as of a father's only son, full of grace and truth. (John 1:14)

Ever since the creation of the world his eternal power and divine nature, invisible though they are, have been understood and seen through the things he has made. (Romans 1:20)

All have sinned and fall short of the glory of God. (Romans 3:23)

I consider that the sufferings of this present time are not worth comparing with the glory about to be revealed to us. (Romans 8:18)

You were bought with a price; therefore glorify God in your body. (1 Corinthians 6:20)

All of us, with unveiled faces, seeing the glory of the Lord as though reflected in a mirror, are being transformed into the same image from one degree of glory to another; for this comes from the Lord, the Spirit. (2 Corinthians 3:18)

For it is the God who said, "Let light shine out of darkness," who has shone in our hearts to give the light of the knowledge of the glory of God in the face of Jesus Christ. (2 Corinthians 4:6)

And this is my prayer, that your love may overflow more and more with knowledge and full insight, to help you determine what is best, so that in the day of Christ you may be pure and blameless, having produced the harvest of righteousness that comes through Jesus Christ for the glory and praise of God. (Philippians 1:9–11)

... and every tongue confess that Jesus Christ is Lord, to the glory of God the Father. (Philippians 2:11)

He is the reflection of God's glory and the exact imprint of God's very being. (Hebrews 1:3a)

You are worthy, our Lord and God, to receive glory and honor and power, for you have created all things, and by your will they existed and were created. (Revelation 4:11)

And the city has no need of sun or moon to shine on it, for the glory of the Lord is its light, and its lamp is the Lamb. (Revelation 21:23)

What to Do

Give glory to God!

Consider: What is the best posture for prayer? Do you like to kneel? ... clasp your hands? ... bow your head? ... lift your heart? ...

Go the distance—prayer is a journey! What does it mean to be "on a journey"?

Let the power of Christ draw you in.

Let your self be transformed.

Sing: "Changed from glory into glory till in heaven we take our place.

Till we cast our crowns before Thee, lost in wonder, love, and praise."
(From the hymn "Love Divine, All Loves Excelling")

A Prayer

Almighty God, You call on us to do all things for Your glory. Help us do so. Our first purpose is to give you glory. Make us able to live in such a way that this is proven in our lives. Make every step I take manifest my trust in Your power and reveal Your kingdom. I ask this prayer in Jesus's Name. Amen.

A Poem

How can I, a fallen soul,
Rise up to meet the glorious goal
    Of giving glory to my Lord,
Who dwells in splendor—pure and whole—
And with His hand yields all control,
      And yet gives me the sweet reward
        To lift my heart before His Throne
        And offer praises of my own?

But I am privileged and glad
To step up now and try to add
    A word of happy gratitude
Because I know that I have had
Great blessings—strong and ironclad—
    For I have truly been renewed
        And I can say that I have known
        The peace that only God has shown.

        And I can say that this will be
        My purpose till eternity.

CONCLUSION

Pray in the Spirit at all times in every prayer and supplication.
—Ephesians 6:18a

Rejoice in hope; be patient in tribulation;
be constant in prayer.
—Romans 12:12

Silence in Prayer

There is "a time to keep silence" (Ecclesiastes 3:7b). In silence there can be a stillness—"Be still and know that I am God" (Psalm 46:10). In silence there can be a peace, a sense of how God is our refuge, our protector, our shield. We need silence. As much as people can pray *we* and *us*, it is not wrong to focus on *me* sometimes. Often silence is waiting. Think of going to see the doctor. Lots of waiting there. "Wait for the Lord; be strong, and let your heart take courage; wait for the Lord" (Psalm 27:14).

There is also a relevance in spending time in solitude. Alone, it is often easier to be silent. It may seem that there are fewer distractions. I will admit, though, not in my head. My mind is often playing music, singing songs, hearing the world. Even in my big empty home, when I am silent, the clock keeps ticking. If the furnace or air conditioner is on, my world is not silent. But importantly, *I* am silent.

But sometimes God reaches out to us with "a still, small voice" (1 Kings 19:12 NKJV). Elijah sought the Lord, desperately. God passed by him on a mountain. At first, there was a great wind, followed by an earthquake, and then a fire. But God was not in these. Finally, there was "a sound of sheer silence" (1 Kings 19:12 NRSV). It seems amazing how, after such disastrous experiences like these, that the silence seems so profound. Even in music, there are moments of silence, scored as a rest note. It's like the composer is preparing listeners to get ready; something special is about to come. If you play records or CDs, often there is silence between tracks from one song or piece of music to the next. And in that silence, there is anticipation. We do not struggle; we do not fear, but our expectations rise.

The dramatic effect of silence can be inspiring. But silence can also seem boring. And most people don't appreciate boredom. We want action. We've gotten used to being busy. We want something to happen, especially when we've been praying. But, who knows, the seed in the soil is surrounded by silence. The moment comes soon when roots and shoots sprout—life! But what is "soon" for me, may seem like "forever" to you.

How do you wait? When I'm in the checkout line, I usually look around or watch the cashier. I'll spend an hour picking out groceries and then expect to check out in one minute. Prayer can seem like there is as much, if not more (way more), waiting. I often pray in words, sentences, making my requests. I almost try to be articulate. But I also just hold my thoughts before God's light, especially when I don't really know exactly what to ask. But as I said in the introduction, prayer is like presenting ourselves to the presence of God.

In Romans 12:12, Paul suggests that we should "be constant in prayer." I don't think he means that we are supposed to pray constantly, all the time, incessantly, but whenever we can. This *can* be "all the time," but we don't want prayer to be burdensome. Sometimes we can be done praying. Our prayers are finished. Of course, if you think about it, we're never really finished. There is always something God sends to our hearts. When I think I am done, somehow, I am often reminded that I could lift our world leaders, all who govern, those in business shaping the world of finance, etc.

When will I be done praising God? Paul said we should "rejoice in hope." The things I hope for are abundant. But ultimately, my prayers for God's kingdom to come cover all of them.

In Ephesians 6:18, Paul encourages us to "pray in the Spirit at all times." I tend to think that when I am praying, I am "in the Spirit." But when I am praying out of my obligation to pray, sometimes I'm not as "in the Spirit" as I want to be. And usually that is when I just hold my thoughts up to God's light, and that usually gets me "in the Spirit." And then, I keep on praying.

The Lord's Prayer is a natural source for a life of prayer. It can ignite a fire within us, and then all we need to do is add fuel, and the fire keeps burning, giving more light, keeping us warm. It feeds us, and we're hungry. We may not think we are, but we should never completely stop feeding ourselves.

The glory of God is our reason for prayer. Our Brother, Jesus, joins us (or invites us to join Him), and with Him we can know God as *our* Father. And by praying, God is able to reach out to us, to embrace us, to move us both outside of ourselves and deeper within. And when we've made our requests, we wait gladly and silently for God to answer.

Amen. It is as it's said when it's said as the truth.

Scriptures

To discover more about what the Bible says about prayer and silence, here are some scripture passages that will help to inspire us:

> Do not be afraid; stand firm, and see the deliverance that the Lord will accomplish for you today; for the Egyptians whom you see today you shall never see again. The Lord will fight for you, and you have only to keep still. (Exodus 14:13–14)

> Be still before the Lord, and wait patiently for him. (Psalm 37:7)

> For God alone my soul waits in silence, for my hope is from him. (Psalm 62:5)

> Set a guard over my mouth, O Lord; keep watch over the door of my lips. (Psalm 141:3)

He was oppressed and he was afflicted, yet he did not open his mouth; like a lamb that is led to the slaughter, and like a sheep that before its shearers is silent, so he did not open his mouth. (Isaiah 53:7)

The Lord is good to those who wait for him, to the soul that seeks him. It is good that one should wait quietly for the salvation of the Lord. (Lamentations 3:25–26)

The Lord is in his holy temple; let the earth keep silence before him. (Habakkuk 2:20)

Be silent before the Lord God! For the day of the Lord is at hand. (Zephaniah 1:7)

But Jesus was silent. (Matthew 26:63)

When the Lamb opened the seventh seal, there was silence in heaven for half an hour. (Revelation 8:1)

What to Do

Spend some time in silence every day. No distractions. Just you and God.

Be still and know that God is God.

Consider: For what do you feel anticipation?

Think of how prayer can sometimes be a way of holding your thoughts in God's light.

Consider: What can add fuel to your spiritual fire?

Respond to the invitation of our Brother who has encouraged us to pray to God as our Father.

A Prayer

Almighty God, before You, words are just wind. We speak, sometimes, just to hear our own voices. You know our hearts and the requests we will make, and yet, we believe You want us to talk to You. So help what we say give praise to Your reign, and give us a heart that will honor Your grace. This we pray in Jesus's Name. Amen.

A Poem

I Will Be Silent Now
I will be silent now and I will just wait,
And gladly will I, then, accept any fate—
Any outcome or fallout of all I request—
And even more will I treasure the ways I am blest.
It's just such a joy to descend with my mind
Into my heart where the purpose I find
Is divine, it's inspired, it makes me feel whole.
It's worth it to see all that stirs in my soul.

Ignite in us all such a glorious fire
That we'll all dream together with a single desire.

My prayers are a journey of peace and of praise,
And the wonderful power that is filling my days
Is the sweetest of nectars, the best of delights.
It is bliss in the morning and love through my nights.

It is as it's said when it's said as the truth. Amen.

Printed in the United States
by Baker & Taylor Publisher Services